Private Property and the Goddess

By Paul Richards, PhD

"I accuse private property of depriving us of everything."
Roque Dalton, Acta/Act

ESTUARY PRESS

First Edition, 2023
ISBN 979-8-9887747-1-6
eBook ISBN 978-1-7344042-5-8
Library of Congress Control Number 2022901865

Cover and Book Design: Paul Richards. Background cover photo from https://wallpapercave.com/w/wp4726006. Venus of Willendorf image from https://www.cleanpng.com.

Published by Estuary Press
472 Skyline Drive
Vallejo, CA 94591

Dedication: For my mother, Hodee Edwards.

Acknowledgments: I wish to thank Nina Serrano for her support and editorial input throughout the writing of this book. Thanks also to Susan Sherrell for help and encouragement. I want to acknowledge the influence of my mother's two long ago publications, *Labor Aristocracy, Mass Base of Social Democracy* (1978, Aurora Press) and *Anatomy of Revisionism* (1979, Aurora Press) for helping me see what was in front of my face.

Contents

Introduction: Mother Earth vs. Patriarchal Private Property

A large framework of ideas about history, prehistory, evolution, and religion arose in front of me in my seventh decade of life. A new world view emerged from my personal evolution as a carpenter-intellectual in the USA. I realized that patriarchal private property stands between us and the Earth, buttressing our mania of destroying her and blocking us from finding our way back to respecting and loving her. It comes down to Mother Earth vs. patriarchal private property. My awareness of this dichotomy arose as I witnessed how humanity is wedded to patriarchy and private property, two sides of the same coin. When I started to explore how this came about, I was headed down a decades-long path to discover the Goddess.

Our embrace of private property blinds us to the mystery of the Goddess. When I say Goddess, I am not referring to a god in the sky. For me, the Goddess is not a force outside of us directing our thoughts or actions. The Goddess is the female source of all life on our beautiful blue planet. Every human culture before patriarchal civilization seems to have understood that. I realized that patriarchal civilization itself is built upon the suppression of the Goddess which includes the oppression of women and the destruction of the natural world.

How do we end our blindness to the Earth? Trying to find the answer to this question started for me with American Indian leader Russell Means' 1980 speech "For America to Live, Europe Must Die." Russell Means (1939-2012) was a leader of the American Indian Movement (AIM) during the occupation of Wounded Knee on the Sioux Indian reservation in 1973. He challenged European Americans generally, but pointedly included Marxists, to respect Mother Earth. He said that European Americans, including Marxists, had proved ourselves unable to hear him. I considered myself a Marxist for many decades so his challenge hit home.

I did not read Russell Means' 1980 speech until well into the new millennium. Things that had never interested me before became obsessions. I started reading in archaeology, genetics, prehistory and Greek mythology. Years passed as I shifted from one subject to the next trying to understand the general crisis of civilization that I have been living in my whole life. When my ideas began to crystallize, I realized that my understanding evolved in the context of my own personal history.

The fact that Means included Marxism in his challenge had a big impact on my thinking. I started to reevaluate Marxism. (See Part 4: Where Marx and Engels Went Wrong.) I would not, however, join the chorus of boos heaped upon it by today's mainstream. If Marxism had become part of the problem, I had to understand it and make some changes.

It was clear that Means was speaking to us across a divide as big as the Grand Canyon, a divide that separates the old paradigm we are now living in from a new one in the process of formation. The old paradigm, based on such biblical ideas as human dominion over the Earth, is now giving way to an understanding that to reestablish a balanced and sustainable way of life requires humans to give up dominion and absolute obedience to the laws of private property. I was on a journey to discover the Goddess who was buried deeply under thick layers of time and denial.

My approach to these ideas arose from my life living outside the mainstream, the left handed, red haired stepchild, son of communists and an interracial family. Over my lifetime, I was dragged along by the mainstream, always aware of my place outside it. Except for my gender identity, which was part of what drove me to dig deeper into Mean's challenge. At first it was a male only conversation. I quickly hit a dead end, however, as I opened my eyes to the role of women in our history and in the rise of civilization. (See Part 1: Private Property, and Part 2: The Circle of the People.)

Seeing that Means had not included the oppression of women in his challenge to Europeans, I embarked on an inquiry into this void. I discovered that female centered human cultures preceded all civilizations. (See Part 3: Women Centered World of Prehistory.) I became aware that human culture evolved with women at the center in prehistory, a time characterized by the absence of private property and war.

Then I explored civilization's mythologies, Greek mythology and the Bible, and saw that they actually chronicled how the current paradigm arose through the suppression of women. This became the key to understanding the relationship between private property and the oppression of women. The rise of private property (the act of seizing the land) destroyed the female centered world that preceded it. This new framework solidified as I toured the ancient origin myths of our culture, the Greek myths as told by Hesiod, and Genesis, chapter one of the Bible. I found that the fight against the influence of the Goddess lay behind everything. (See Part 5: Greek Myths, and Part 6: Patriarchy's One God of the Bible.)

The Goddess was the elephant in the room during the rise of civilization. And now, private property is the elephant in the room during the rise of a new paradigm.

In my conclusion (Chapter 37: Can We Live in Harmony with Nature?), I confess to believing that we can live in harmony with nature. We have the means and the understanding to do it. Private property stands in the way.

Part 1: Private Property

1: Russell Means Challenge

"There is the traditional Lakota way and the ways of the American Indian peoples. It is the way that knows that humans do not have the right to degrade Mother Earth, that there are forces beyond anything the European mind has conceived, that humans must be in harmony with all relations or the relations will eventually eliminate the disharmony." [1]

Means made it very clear: "Humans do not have the right to degrade Mother Earth." Then he said: "American Indians have been trying to explain this to Europeans for centuries. But, ... Europeans have proven themselves unable to hear."

Being of European descent, I felt I had to listen to him and to respond to his legitimate questions. I did not want to refute him or to justify myself. In my mind, I respected nature. But obviously this is not enough.

As a life long socialist who believes that a better, more humane world is possible, I was especially challenged by what Means had to say about Marxism.

So, in order for us to really join forces with Marxism, we American Indians would have to accept the national sacrifice of our homeland; we would have to commit cultural suicide and become industrialized and Europeanized. . . .

Revolutionary Marxism, like industrial society in other forms, seeks to "rationalize" all people in relation to industry — maximum industry, maximum production. It is a materialist doctrine that despises the American Indian spiritual tradition, our cultures, our lifeways. Marx himself called us "precapitalists" and "primitive." Precapitalist simply means that, in his view, we would eventually discover capitalism and become capitalists; we have always been economically retarded in Marxist terms. The only manner in which American Indian people could participate in a Marxist revolution would be to join the industrial system, to become factory workers, or "proletarians," as Marx called them. The man was very clear about the fact that his revolution could occur only through the struggle of the proletariat, that the existence of a massive industrial system is a precondition of a successful Marxist society.

I think there is a problem with language here. Christians, capitalists, Marxists. All of them have been revolutionary in their own minds, but none of them really means revolution. What they really mean is a continuation. They do what they do in order that European culture can continue to exist and develop according to its needs.[2]

Means asserts that Marxists seek a continuation of the industrial system, which to him, standing outside the industrial system, makes it non-revolutionary by definition. For an American Indian, an indigenous person seeking harmony with the natural world, the industrial system itself is the problem. Revolution for an indigenous person is not, according to Means, about making the industrial world more democratic. It is about making it compatible with a healthy planet and the continued existence of indigenous peoples and their cultures. In today's modern civilizations, we cannot conceive of life without the industrial system. Russell Means demands that we evaluate revolutionary ideas from the standpoint of their impact on non-European peoples. He rejects completely the idea that indigenous people should give up their cultures, their languages, and their lands for any reason, especially in order to join the proletariat or merge into the industrial system in any form.

Where is the Goddess?

Women and the Goddess do not appear explicitly in his challenge, directed to Christians, capitalists and Marxists, gender-less terms like "man" that might refer to all sexes. At first, this linguistic framework shaped my inquiry by default. My journey started within the non gendered framework of the English language. Bringing the Goddess into Russell Means' call to respect nature appeared as a distraction, pulling me away from my central inquiry. When I first encountered his challenge, the implications of a gender-less discussion were not apparent to me. Putting gender and the Goddess into the discussion seemed as impossible as trying to conceive of a world outside the industrial system. Yet, putting gender into it was unavoidable since without it, the discussion went nowhere. Without understanding the Goddess and role of gender in history and prehistory, I was left with the dismal prospect of "Europe must die." Period.

In our culture when we say "man" we think we mean people, men and women. But really it means men. Every culture has its own language and its own term for "people." In European culture, the term for people is man. And that is no accident. It is fundamental. As a man reading Russell Means' challenge, I was on familiar ground and could proceed without adding gender to the conversation. Most women in the room would, at this point, lose interest, gaze out the window and look at their watches. It was a familiar framework for me as a male intellectual. The active participants in such a discussion kept narrowing down. "Europe must die" left most men behind. Excluding gender from the discussion left most women out too. But, still, I accepted his challenge and pushed ahead anyway not realizing that eventually it would lead me to the Goddess.

I realized that Means' challenge to European culture was not some philosophical hair splitting like between Adam Smith and Karl Marx about the labor theory of value. Adam Smith and Karl Marx had a dispute very much within western patriarchal culture. Their argument was like two men arm wrestling in a bar. Whoever wins the contest does not change the basic context. How does the contest relate to non-Europeans? How does it relate to the previous occupants of the land on which the bar was built, the trees cut down, the hops grown for the beer they drink, the water they appropriated? And how does it relate to the barmaid serving the beer?

The arm wrestlers might look up from their contest and shout, "Manifest Destiny! We won. You lost. Now get over it." That kind of response only worked until the planet started to heat up, the air turned brown, and the water became undrinkable. This kind of denial has a harder time standing up to scrutiny these days, especially after native people and women found their voices in law schools, journalism, and politics. The great claim to European superiority over the original inhabitants of the land has become a self serving notion based on the lie that the land was empty, that we (read men) had a right to it and that European patriarchal ways were the best. The planetary crisis has invalidated all these notions.

When I came across Russell Means challenge to Marxism it gave rise to a question I had never asked myself: Was there ever a time when my people, European and Jewish people, lived like the tribes that Russell Means spoke for? Was there a time when my ancestors might have lived in harmony with nature? How far back would I have to go to find such a time, if it ever existed at all? How did we lose respect for the natural world and for women?

I could not answer that question for others unless I could answer it for myself. For most of my life, I have been one of those Europeans who is unable to hear the call to respect nature. The only way I could explore our blindness was to examine my own blindness and the decades long path to my own awakening, an awakening that came with my increasing isolation in this society. My search had to start with my mother, Hodee (nee) Waldstein, and my father, Harvey Richards.

2: **My Ancestors Were Settlers**

Responding to Russell Means set off a dialog in my mind between me, as a descendant of the settler/conquerors, and Indigenous people. This dialog woke me up to the fact that in spite of all my radicalism over my whole life, I was speaking for the conquerors. Not out of a conscious choice, since I had always been a dissenter. But I was speaking for them because I am their descendant and I occupy the land my ancestors conquered. I realized that the settler mindset is built into modern society, and into me, simply as I live a modern life handed down to me by my ancestors. I knew then that I would not find a time in all of history when my ancestors lived in harmony with nature. I would have to look before and beyond history.

On My Father's Side

On my father's mother's side (Norma Baker Richardson was my grandmother's name) my great great grandfather, John Baker, settled in Oregon in the 1840's. He served in the wars against the tribes of the Rogue River Valley before Oregon became a state in 1859. He was granted 253 acres of land in what is now Salem, Oregon, for his service. That is my heritage. My father grew up in Salem, Oregon.

Generations passed and the land was quickly sold off, lost as succeeding generations left the farm. I grew up not knowing about John Baker at all, so my debt to him was not even visible to me. Nevertheless, my current happy ownership of my home and lot today in California would never have happened without such wars of conquest that displaced the tribes and established the settler laws and powers over the land we all live on. The land grant was given to soldier John Baker, not to his wife. The spoils of war and the benefits of civilization begin with the wars to seize the land and displace its original inhabitants. Not knowing about John Baker did not change the facts of the matter for me or everyone else around me.

I found out about John Baker in the 1980's when my father handed me a large brown envelope his mother, Norma, left with him. It contained 10 handwritten pages in small script outlining what she knew about our ancestors. It went back to John Baker, her grandfather, who came across the continent in a covered wagon in the 1840's. His service in the wars against the Oregon tribes left no doubt about how patriarchal private property impacted my family. And even though no one in my immediate family, my father or grandmother, ever to my knowledge received a dime from this land grant, it clearly identifies us as descendants who benefited directly from the conquest.

On my father's father's side, on the Richards side of the family, my ancestors go back to Robert Richards of Somerset, England. He came across the Atlantic in the 1840's to Wisconsin, not long after the Black Hawk war of 1832 against the Sac and Fox tribes who were trying unsuccessfully to move back to their homelands. His son, also named Robert Richards, fought for the Union during the Civil War and was wounded in Mississippi. I am proud to be descended from a veteran of the Union side of the Civil War, from a man who spilled his blood to end slavery and save the Union. But I realized that during our civil war, President Lincoln authorized the largest mass hanging in our history when, on December 26, 1862, following the U.S.-Dakota War of 1862, the federal government hanged 38 members of the Dakota tribe in Minnesota, the largest mass execution in United States history. The victory of the Union meant something completely different to the tribes than it meant to me.

I know very little about my ancestors before these great great grandfathers. But for the purposes of my search for a time when my ancestors might have lived in harmony with nature, it doesn't seem to matter whether I know about them or not. Knowing about my paternal lineage is enough to focus my search on my roots in the history of the US and England.

On My Mother's Side

My mother's maiden name was Hodee Waldstein. I knew little about the Waldstein and Frank (her mother's maiden name) since my mother was alienated from them and hardly ever mentioned them. I knew I had cousins back east to whom she sent the clothes I grew out of. I knew I had a cousin named Danny whose photo as a baby I had seen. I also knew he went to war in Vietnam and that closed the door completely on the possibility of us ever meeting. My isolation from family fit perfectly into my mother's aloofness that spanned the time from morning to night and from my earliest memories to the end of her life in 2012. It was all but impossible for me to look into my mother's side of the family with our Jewish roots going back to immigrants from Poland and Lithuania in the 1880s. I had to cross a deep and wide canyon of hidden rejections that went back generations.

Hodee worked at various jobs throughout the time I was growing up. I was a latch key kid, carrying the house key on a chain around my neck so I could get into the house after school. She was a secretary and a scientific catalog writer as well as a journalist for the People's World, the west coast Communist newspaper. She had spent a year in graduate school at Bryn Mawr College as well as four years at Radcliffe obtaining a degree in physics. She left that career path when she joined the Communist Party and married my father back east before arriving in San Francisco. She was also a talented and developed violin player. She kept her violin in the closet and never brought it out. Ever.

When I was growing up in the 1950's, she carried this past silently and sullenly. The Old Testament was part of the cultural heritage that my mother had rejected totally and fled from, including fleeing from her family. She rejected her parent's world, including their religion, and kept us children away from it, 3,000 miles away from Boston and her relatives, including her mother and sisters whom we never met until I was grown up. I look at it now with the realization that we were part of a patriarchal ethnic group trying to find a place among surrounding hostile patriarchal settler societies in Europe and North America.

It would have been convenient for me to have believed in the male God of the Old Testament in my later struggle to obtain conscientious objector status to avoid the draft. But that never occurred to me. My Jewish roots were far away, separated from me by a vast empty space that separated my mother and her family. My share of this isolation led me to ask where were my cousins? My grandmother? Why were we so alone? I can see now that the Old Testament, the handbook of patriarchy, was fundamental to the problems. My isolation and pain gave me the motivation to keep on digging, helping in the writing of this book.

How could I not reject out of hand the Bible's assertion that the Earth began 6,000 years ago? Religious faith in this kind of assertion blocks any rational inquiry into our prehistoric roots which, it became very clear, is where my search had to go to find answers. The Bible makes asking questions about our prehistoric roots a kind of blasphemy. My search for a time when my ancestors were indigenous had to look into the forbidden prehistory 6000 years ago, before the Bible was written, before God allegedly created the Earth. So I chose to focus on my father's side.

Looking at Britain

Us Richards came from England, Wales, Cornwall and Somerset where the Richards ancestors lived back in the 18th century. Somerset with its rich archaeological record offered me a glimpse into the prehistory of my roots, even before the Richards migrated into Somerset from Wales (Richards being a Welsh name.)

The people of the British Isles today are descendants of our prehistory, one of the most looked at and thought about prehistories on Earth. Prehistoric artifacts appear almost anywhere you dig a hole in the ground on the British Isles. The people of the United Kingdom (the home of the Industrial Revolution) share responsibility for the disasters taking place on our planet as much or more than any other modern nation. Those of us in the USA who descend from them are equally playing out the legacy of the culture that arose from the prehistory of the British isles and Europe. And it is here that I focus my search for the time when my ancestors were not settlers.

Russell Means' challenge to Europeans to respect nature was specifically directed at Marxists such as myself. In all my university years studying history, my focus on Marxism had blinded me to the inherent bias of the settler mindset in me. Ironically, at the time I was a graduate student in History at the University of Wisconsin, Madison, I never realized that my great great grandfather, Robert Richards, had lived 20 miles west of me. My studies were about remote people all over the world, but not about my people 20 miles to the west. Examining my own blindness became an important step in my inquiry.

3: Marxism in My Blood

Marxism entered my life early growing up as a red diaper baby in Oakland, California. My parents were part of the Communist movement in the US. I followed their lead in joining radicals, communists and rebels at every turn throughout my life. I embraced civil disobedience in the 1960's, sitting in for civil rights and went to jail in San Francisco for two months. I resisted the draft, refusing to go to Vietnam. Years and years of marching in ever larger demonstrations against war and for peace and justice, however, did not change the world the way I had hoped. My country continued to make war, to oppress workers, people of color, and, most especially, women and indigenous tribes. The streets remained the same, concrete and dirty, filled with dangers. As I grew older, my participation in politics over the years petered out, ending in silence and isolation. My Marxism remained, however.

I lived as an isolated radical in a hostile world. Marxism became more and more remote to my actual life, like a memory slipping away into the past. But at first, early in my awareness as a child, it was not remote. Even not understanding what it was, Marxism slipped into my life through my parent's lives, much like a religion did in other families. My father had been a classic Marxist worker radical of the 1930's and 40's. He was a communist organizer with an 8th grade education, working as a machinist in the San Francisco shipyards, a rank and file activist, and a shop steward during the 1946 west coast strike. He carried the weight of the radical left into the post war world along with a gun in his pocket. I knew nothing of this as a two year old, of course, which was when my parents separated and then divorced. As Harvey's family fell apart, so did the rest of his world. He was fired from his job, expelled from his union, and exiled from his trade. He was a victim of the settlement of the 1946 west coast machinist strike that gave some wage concessions to the workers in exchange for expelling communists from the Machinists Union. A bad deal that killed the unions, which, as my father said, were worthless without their militants.

I was also unaware as a four year old that my mother and African American step father, George Edwards, were married in 1948 in a state where interracial marriage was illegal. They had to take a train to Washington state to tie the knot. George had to carry their marriage license with them to prevent being arrested for "white slavery" which is what authorities could charge any black man who had the nerve to travel across state lines with a white woman.

My First Jobs

As I grew up and found my first jobs, I did not follow in my father's footsteps in a mass production industrial labor force. I took up carpentry working with a Quaker pacifist guy doing home remodeling out of the back of his pick up truck. I learned my trade from him and never wanted to find work with big companies that were unionized. I worked my way through school that way, all the way to a PhD. And then, I left academia for the construction trades, leaving the diplomas hanging on my wall above the tool boxes out of which I made a living.

My only experience with employment in a mass industry occurred during my undergraduate days in Berkeley, 1961 to 1966, in the warehouses of the East Bay where I found work through the International Longshore and Warehouse Union local 10. I got warehouse jobs through my radical friends' parents who held office in the union and could sneak me in through the backdoor of the hiring hall. I worked as a student, part time, in drug store warehouses. Everyone in the warehouse knew I was somebody's relative or friend, which was how summer hiring took place in those days. Humping cases, as the work was called, was really boring. The old timers looked at me during lunch time and told me nicely to "Get the hell out of here." They were counting off the years until retirement and hated the work. It was no place for a young man going to college, they said. I followed their advice but went into construction instead.

So what was Marxism to a guy like me? I guess if there had been a Marxist church, I could have attended on weekends to fit into the pattern of other religions in the community. But, of course, the only Marxist church was the Communist Party which was stuck firmly in the past especially during its death throws in the McCarthy witch hunt days of the 1950s. So instead, I just held my tongue and buried my real radical self in silence inside me.

Social Impact of Anti-Communism

I experienced the demise of the Communist Party (CP) personally during my childhood in the deteriorating relationships between the communist families that I grew up around. A terrible silence arose among us as the persecution against the Party spread and deepened. The CP had a rule that you were never to speak to the FBI and if you were contacted by them you were supposed to report it to the CP leaders. When the CP went "underground", my mother and African American step father refused to go along with them. Going "underground" meant that the leaders went into hiding. My mother and step father found this laughable and left the party. My father participated in it, ferrying the clandestine leaders by car around the state. Once while driving them through California's central valley, the car was stopped by the police and everyone in it was arrested, except my father. From then on he was considered untrustworthy and so ended his association with the CP.

But just because you were no longer in the CP was no reason for the FBI to stop harassing you. When I was in grammar school, living with my mother and stepfather, we moved frequently because the FBI intimidated our landlords who then evicted us. My mother went from job to job because the FBI intimidated her employers and they fired her. This constant moving from house to house and from job to job took its toll. Finally in the late 1950's, my mother decided to accept the invitation to talk with the FBI to try to stop their harassment. Of course, the FBI was not impressed with her as she refused to talk about anyone else and so the meeting did no good. However, even though she was no longer in the CP, she reported the FBI contact to the party. The CP then deemed her even more untrustworthy, driving the wedge deeper between her and her former comrades. This kind of pressure split apart many families, who were at one time friends and comrades into isolated and bitter family groups who merged into the poor and displaced elements of society around them. Certainly it was a victory for the FBI and the anti-communist crusaders.

In the summer of 1961, my mother and stepfather sat me down one evening to tell me that they planned to move to Ghana, West Africa. Shocked and surprised, I asked them, "When?" "Next month," they said. I had just graduated high school, and now here they were leaving for Africa. My world had suddenly gone global, no longer confined to my Oakland neighborhood. George had been laid off from his plumbing job of 10 years after his boss learned he planned to move away. They didn't have a lot of money, so they told me they had to sell the house, cars, and the furniture to get the plane tickets. My head was spinning. Very soon, people, including some old comrades, began stopping by to pick up furniture, the hi-fi set, the couch, chairs, TV, beds and so on. It was a garage sale with strange people nosing around the house touching things, whispering, and finally lugging things out the front door to their cars and trucks.

Soon I found a room in the back of the house of one of my family's friends in Berkeley and moved there. It was a great relief to be out of the house as it was being picked apart. I returned weekends to help pack up. Questions finally came up in my mind as I thought about what was happening. They told me that they had friends in Los Angeles, other black workers in the building trades, who were moving to Ghana to help the first independent, post-colonial country on the continent. They told me about Kwame Nkrumah, Ghana's leader. They wanted to lend a hand, George as a plumber, and my mother as a writer. My sister was going with them, which was the only thing an 11 year old could do under the circumstances. I was already into my new life as a freshman at UC Berkeley, so their leaving was not going to land me on the street. But it was going to leave a big hole in my world.

More immediately, I wondered who were those people taking all the furniture? What is going to happen to the house? I didn't say it but I thought maybe it might be mine once they left. But then I learned later that George had gambling debts and everything was going to go to pay people off. I even discovered that they gave the house to a friend because they were afraid "leg breakers" might show up to collect old debts once they were gone. So I added up two and two and realized they were running out on their debts. One of the people who showed up to remove our furniture was the barber who had a shop up the street on 23rd Ave in a garage store front. I had my haircut there when I was a small boy. Now I realized it was where George placed his bets. All my childhood images of life in East Oakland faded away into this new grown up reality. And it did not take me long to realize that there would be nothing left once they departed for Africa.

Finally the day arrived for them to go. I drove up to the house in my yellow '57 Chevy and loaded the family, including my sister and all their suitcases into the car. I felt heartbroken to be losing them. But I knew they needed a ride and I was glad I could be the one to take them. It was a dark cold rainy night in December when we drove away from the house to the freeway, over the Bay Bridge and onto Highway 101 to the airport. We said our goodbyes with hugs and kisses and then I turned around and went back to the car. I had told my dad I was coming there to stay the night after dropping everyone off at the airport. When I got there, I went inside and we sat down in their beautiful living room full of nice furniture in wood paneled walls. I told them what I just did and then to my surprise, I wept and wept like I had never done before or since.

View from the Far Left

As a freshman student, I witnessed the movements for change from the standpoint of a radical from a communist family background. I entered college without any career objectives beyond just trying to find out if my radical assumptions about the world would stand up to close examination. I was thrilled to associate myself with the burgeoning movements of radical students who were rocking the world. I ran straight to the picket lines and found friends and associates among the protesters. My red background, however, stayed in the background. Most people in the movement came from the mainstream with all the illusions of the mainstream and all of the shock and disillusionment that came with the youthful discovery of injustice and inequality all around us. For me, it was shocking to see the shock and disillusionment.

In 1961, the University of California required me to sign up for the US Army's Reserve Officers Training Corps, ROTC. I faced a choice of signing up or not going to the University of California. So I signed up. I immediately got active in the "Abolish ROTC" movement. I joined picket lines protesting the compulsory ROTC classes. ROTC classes included wearing the Army's uniforms, issued from big rooms full of supplies in the campus gym, for the practice marches around grassy UC athletic fields. I slogged my way through these classes until my second year when the University abolished compulsory ROTC. This victory went to my head. It seemed as if our little picket lines had brought the US Army to its knees. The sky was the limit, I thought.

At about this time, my father handed me several boxes of books that included the Marxist library from the recently defunct California Labor School, a communist sponsored school for workers in San Francisco. He had worked for the Labor School helping to close it down and brought the books home to his garage. He met Alice Schott Meigs, my future stepmother, there in a class he taught about labor history. The collection of books included three volumes of *Das Kapital*, the complete works of Vladimir Lenin, and other classics of Marxism by Engels, Stalin and others. Ah ha! I said to myself. Now I can find out what all this communist stuff is really all about. I carried them to my apartment in Berkeley and started to read them one by one.

These volumes focused on the role of the proletariat in liberation struggles. Liberation struggles, from my perspective in the US of the 1950s, all seemed to be happening abroad. Workers like my family were increasingly isolated in a racist, conservative society. I grew up among working class families until Verde Valley and then college where I very quickly moved into the middle class world of students. I sat in Marxist study groups of W.E.B. DuBois clubs discussing class struggle with sharp graduate students who seemed to know it all.

Much to my dismay, mainstream conservative arguments dominated my college classes. I remained submerged in my anti-capitalist, pro communist perspective. But even then in the early 1960's, my role as the radical in the room was becoming tiresome.

Very early in my student years at UC Berkeley, I went to work painting student apartments for a guy who had me investigated by his FBI buddies. I learned how to be a painter from him but could not escape the anti-communist mainstream anywhere. Meanwhile, my whole generation signed up for the war in Vietnam and went off to die for country and flag. When I turned 18 in May, 1962, I had gone down to the post office and signed up for the draft, as required at the time. But I never imagined participating in a war like the Vietnam war. My head was full of TV images of World War II anti-fascist glory defeating Hitler and the Nazis. But the world had changed.

It was all very perplexing and discouraging. I would leave a demonstration against the war at the local draft board, go to my painting job with my FBI loving boss, and then return to my apartment full of Marxist books. Both in academia and in my work-a-day world, my radical views separated me from the traditional avenues of advancement which left me sitting way out on a skinny branch.

The Earth Loomed Up

Gradually, the real lessons learned in order to work as a carpenter in the home repair business came to dominate my life. The Earth loomed up before me demanding my attention and careful analysis. Radical world views did not matter in the job market, at least as long as the FBI wasn't around. As long as I stayed under the radar, out of sight in the cash economy, the feds had no idea I existed and that was the way I wanted to keep it. All that mattered was whether you could do the work. This contrasted greatly in my mind to teaching jobs that came along with loyalty oaths.

I had entered into the construction trades with my Quaker carpenter boss and very limited real knowledge. My African American stepfather was a plumber and worked in the construction of the housing tracks that were going up in the post war years here in the Bay Area. He got a plumber's union card without going through the apprenticeship program which was closed to blacks in the 1950s. He took the journeyman's test surreptitiously after an old leftist friend who was the union business agent, let him into the journeyman's exam and he passed it. I had watched him work on plumbing jobs around our house and gained some understanding of the various systems that make up the modern wood frame house. So, working in the trades seemed a natural thing for me.

My attraction to construction, however, was not about finding a mass base and becoming an influential leader among workers. That had been one of the few pieces of advice my father actually offered me. "Find a mass base," he told me. I saw what that did for him. No thanks. I worked for cash in the building trades and could no more claim leadership of other carpenters than I could have provided leadership in that warehouse full of lifers telling me to get the hell out of there. Instead, I followed the lessons my stepfather had left me, learn by doing, earn a living on the periphery, stay under the radar. What started out as a part time supplement for a college student turned into a lifelong trade.

Civil Rights and the Vietnam War

As a freshman in UC Berkeley in 1961, I got active in the civil rights movements by going to SNCC and CORE demonstrations in support of the southern civil rights struggles against legal segregation. Many local students such as myself saw that there were real racial justice issues in the Bay Area that needed to be addressed in addition to the southern struggles. This local focus was especially keen among leftist radicals on campus who had formed the W.E.B. DuBois Clubs and later the Ad Hoc Committee Against Racial Discrimination. Unknown to me at the time as a green freshman, these groups arose out of the Communist Party clubs in Berkeley, Oakland, and San Francisco. Getting active in them placed me squarely inside the old CP circles that my parents had left some years earlier. Radical leftists were the main connection students had with the local community around us. I saw that the communists had separate meetings to discuss events and come up with ideas about what we should do. Much of the outreach for our demonstrations, the goals, publicity, and wording of leaflets came out of these separate meetings. I did not resent it because I saw the value of coherent leadership in all the wildly spontaneous rebellions taking place in those years.

In the summer of 1964, at age 20, I married my Verde Valley high school sweetheart, Susan Alland. She had been with me through all the demonstrations and arrests of the early civil rights movement before the Vietnam war cast its ugly pall over our world. Her parents knew we were too young to marry, but there was no turning us back and we tied the knot. Love and idealism was in the air. "Trust no one over 30" was the mantra of the times. We rushed blindly into our future.

I became a member of the DuBois Clubs but I was not invited to the CP meetings. I watched all this from afar. I could see that the effectiveness of what we were doing was really a product of the behind the scenes coordination and thinking that came out of the communist circles. It gave me an appreciation of how my parents had become communists and what attracted them to that kind of organizing. And I also saw how secrecy in a popular organization opened the door to FBI informants infiltration and manipulation of factions among us. It was an atmosphere of heady idealism undercut with suspicion and back stabbing.

I was president of the Berkeley DuBois club in 1963 at the time we inaugurated the sit-in demonstrations against racial discrimination in hiring at the Sheraton Palace hotel, Mel's Drive-In restaurants, and the auto dealerships in San Francisco. My wife and I got arrested during all three of these struggles. I received the longest jail sentence handed out for breaking trespass laws as we sat in and disrupted businesses until they abandoned their racist hiring practices. My wife refused to let the cops fingerprint her during these arrests which later caused the prosecutors to dismiss all charges against her. These businesses did abandon their racist hiring practices, which of course received very little publicity and did nothing to stop the authorities from jailing all of us who dared to call a halt to them.

Resisting the Draft

In addition to the diploma for my graduation from UC Berkeley in February, 1966, I also received a little brown envelope from the Selective Service with my order to report to the pre-induction physical at the Oakland Army Induction Center. My student deferment had expired. At about that time, I joined the Communist Party. I joined the Party when the draft started breathing down my neck and I quit when the draft finally gave up on me. My association with the Communist Party was my statement to the US Armed Forces at war with world communism. I resisted the draft hoping all the while that the Army would do a security check on me. Putting the CP in my resume was hopefully going to be enough to let them know they did not want me. However, it didn't quite work out that way.

In April, 1966, I went to my pre-induction physical at the Oakland Army Induction Center, where fate threw me a curve ball. I came to the door where the security check was supposed to happen and it was locked. The whole line of draftees in their underwear continued on down the hall to the next station. I stopped there and asked the first uniformed person who came by what was happening with the locked door. He said that the officer who did the security check was out sick that day. I couldn't help wondering if they locked that door specifically for my benefit.

My 1-A classification followed soon after that. It was a good time to visit my mother, stepfather and sister in Ghana, West Africa. There were no US Army bases in Ghana at the time. I informed the draft board that I was in Ghana and they postponed my pre-induction physical until I returned. Sitting in my parent's home in tropical Kumasi in the summer of 1966, I filled out the Selective Service conscientious objector forms I had put into my suitcase on my way to the airport. I planned to create a means of appeal and delay within the Selective Service system. I claimed philosophical Marxism as my reason for not serving in the armed forces. Marxism was not included in the list of religions that might justify conscientious objection to war, however. It did not play well with the draft board neither. It did enable me to file numerous appeals to delay the process again and again.

4: Marxist Conscientious Objector to War

I thought studying in the University would be the place for me to see if my ideals held water. But it turned out that fighting the draft put my ideals to the real test. Conscientious Objector application form 150 forced me to state exactly what my radical ideals were. Now, half a century later, my attempt to get the draft board to exempt me from going to war for "religious" reasons was not as lame as I thought it was when I wrote it. I can see now that it was a long slow contest between men, me vs. the draft board. Patriarchy had its rules of war and made no room for men like me. The all male draft board, appeals boards, courts, prisons, and cops blinded me and everyone else to the Goddess. I had to travel a long road before I would find her.

Many thousands of us resisted the draft. Some burned our draft cards. Others went to Canada, and others went to jail. As prime meat for the war makers at age 23, I had to choose my own path of resistance. My stubborn streak exploded inside me. No matter what the world demanded of me, I knew I would never go into the imperialist army. I envisioned it down to imagining the rooms where I would face my fate. Would it be in the Induction center when they asked me to raise my hand and step forward? Would it be when the police cornered me and took me to jail? Which kind of jail would I go to? Federal, state, or military prison? It was an easy choice. It would be in a civilian prison, not military. No stepping forward, raising my right hand and pledging allegiance for me. They would have to arrest me as a civilian. The question was how long would it take for me to reach this seemingly inevitable doom?

I decided to claim to be a conscientious objector to war figuring all the while that my claims would be rejected. In part I did it to gain access to the draft system's appeals procedures in order to delay the inevitable rejections. As an atheist, I also knew that the religious requirement for conscientious objectors was wrong. It violated the separation of church and state and our right to free speech. I learned this in 1966 doing anti-draft counseling in local high schools in the last months of my student deferment.

I thought about it sitting there in Kumasi, looking at the draft form 150's questions. From the first I knew I would not flee the country for a life as an expatriate. Me and my ideals were as American as apple pie, and no reactionary mainstream would force me out. Mohammad Ali was my role model.

Soon after arriving at my family's home in Kumasi, Ghana, I pulled the CO forms out of my suitcase. I borrowed my mother's typewriter and wrote up my answers in duplicate with carbon paper and onion skin paper below it. It was a very challenging task mainly because I did not want to do it.

> *Question two: Describe the nature of your beliefs which is the basis of your claim made in Series I above, and state whether or not your belief in a Supreme Being involved duties which to you are superior to those arising from any human relation.*

Series I was yes or no, I am "by reason of religious training and belief conscientiously opposed to participation in war in any form." I said yes.

Putting such big questions to young men facing life and death choices was like shooting ducks in a pond for the cynical members of the draft board. No one told me about the 1965 Supreme Court 9 to 0 vote in the US v. Seeger decision that had upheld the right of a non religious draftee to CO status. I was not even aware that it was important to make a case for myself that would have a chance of success in court reviews. I was 23 years old trying to reason out my own true beliefs about life and the world to fit into the little boxes on the Form 150. I wrote:

> *I believe in mankind, in the goodness of man, in the goodness of his potential for love, happiness, and dignity. I have an intense faith, based on my experience during my life and on my study of other countries and peoples and their observations of mankind, that this potential can be, will be, and must be fulfilled. I hold the attainment of this potential as the main purpose for my life. ... This 'calling' I consider to be my supreme duty to which all else is subordinate.*

> *In my experience I have understood a Supreme Being to be many things to many people; it is one thing to a Christian, another to a Jew, and quite another to a Buddhist. My belief is in humanity and its destiny. I believe in this as strongly as one who believes in a Supreme Being of a more traditional sort. My belief in my Supreme Being and my duties towards it requires absolute fidelity*

and integrity on my part. This means to me that any human relation which may arise (such as my "obligation" to serve in the U.S. Army) that contradicts my beliefs must remain subordinate to my duty to do what I see as right and good.

It was a tortured statement trying to fit my Marxist beliefs into the framework of the religious assumptions built into the draft law. Looking at it now, many decades later, I can see that the fight against the Vietnam war and the draft consolidated my world view in my mind so I could interpolate it into Form 150. My years at UC Berkeley, along with the sit ins, jail, and activist study groups—all precipitated these grandiose statements. I can also see that I fit squarely into the European cultural framework with "man" at its center. My Marxism had no trouble fitting into the little boxes on the form 150, even though I was pushing the limits and fighting the system. When I finished writing it, I was greatly relieved. I put it in an envelope ready to submit it at my first opportunity.

My African adventure could not go on forever. I was not looking for a life as an exile. My wife had accompanied me on the African visit. We decided to take a tour of Europe on our way home to face the music. We spent a month visiting Rome, Berlin, Prague, and then Paris. Then, while sipping coffee in a Paris cafe in July, 1966, I received a letter from my lawyer telling me that our legal appeals of the sentences for sitting in against racist hiring practices had finally failed. Two hundred or so of the other demonstrators were already in jail serving their sentences. "It is time to bite the bullet," my lawyer wrote to me. So we flew back from Paris landing me in the San Francisco county jail in San Bruno, locked up in a pale green cell. Surrendering to the police to serve that sentence was one of the saddest moments of my life.

San Francisco County Jail

As deeply satisfying as it was to confront and destroy such racist hiring practices in a few businesses, the two months I spent in San Francisco county jail changed my life forever. When I got off the plane from Europe on our way back from Ghana, my wife Susan and I went to my father's house quietly to shed our jet lag for a few days before I surrendered myself to the San Francisco sheriff to serve my two months in jail. I really did not want to do it but there was no way out. I went into San Francisco to my lawyer's office to surrender. We walked from his office over to the City Hall slowly talking about nothing in particular.

The court house had marble lined corridors and wood paneled court rooms. We entered one courtroom where my lawyer shook hands cordially with a prosecutor guy. Soon a deputy emerged from a door in the wood paneling and took me back into the non-public part of the court where there was no wood paneling, no marble, just light green painted walls and concrete with neutral colored linoleum floors. Before I knew it I had emptied my pockets, removed my belt and shoe laces and was locked into a large cell on the top floor of the courthouse with several other men to await transport by bus to San

Bruno where the San Francisco county jail was located. The bus had bars over all the windows and big signs on the sides of the bus "San Francisco City and County". All the cars on the freeway passed us by oblivious to us prisoners as I looked wistfully out the window at them.

In San Bruno, we got off the bus and walked into the basement of a six story concrete building. I surrendered the rest of my clothes and stood naked in front of a jailer who issued me underwear, jailhouse one piece coveralls two sizes too small and some horrible brown leather shoes. I put these items down on a bench in the next room and was ordered to walk through a shallow pond of some terrible liquid to kill off some alleged germs in my feet. Then I was sprayed with a white powder everywhere front and back and bend over and spread em. I pointed out to the jailer that the coveralls were too small. "Tough shit" was his response. Since I couldn't get them up over my shoulders, I just zipped them part way up and tied the arms around my waist. With a blanket and a suspicious looking pillow I was escorted up some stairs to the first floor rotunda, a large space that was six stories high.

The rotunda opened up to two wings, one on each side. The left side of the first floor was the all white dorm. The right side was the all black dorm. I nodded briefly to a couple of the other demonstrators who were walking through the rotunda as I arrived. We then walked up two flights of stairs to a cell on the third floor south where all newly arriving inmates were placed. I was placed in a single cell, 6 feet by

8 feet, with concrete walls, a metal bed and a toilet and sink. The cell doors banged shut in unison with a loud bang from a central control.

I awoke on that first morning in jail to a guard who threw a brown envelope through the bars onto the floor. It was addressed to me from the Selective Service. Greetings, it began. Some inmate down the hall yelled out, laughing loudly, "They want your ass!" General snickering followed.

It was my order to report for duty in the Army. On the back of the form was a list of reasons why you could not make it. One of them was "I am in jail." I checked that box and sent it in. They postponed my induction and as soon as I got out of jail, I filed the conscientious objector applications I had written up in Africa. The next day, I was assigned a bed in the white dorm.

The first time I went downstairs to take a shower, I placed my clothes on a chair only to find them missing when I came out of the shower to dry off. No one knew anything about it, of course, so I had to walk through the jail up a flight of stairs to the office wrapped in a towel to report my missing clothes so they would issue me a new set. At least I got rid of the dam coveralls. I was issued jeans, a shirt and new underwear. I thought how similar issuing jail clothes was to issuing uniforms in the ROTC classes I had been required to take a few years earlier.

I got accustomed to the routines quickly enough. There was the usual stuff like work times, free times, yard times and night times. They counted everyone twice a day, morning and night. You were locked into your cell at night and let into the hallway in the morning. The cell doors remained open during the day.

I soon discovered that the 250 or so demonstrators in the jail of 800 inmates had started a campaign to desegregate the jail. After a day or so I was assigned a job in the front office to do typing. I received a nicely ironed collared shirt and fresh pressed jeans along with it. I listened to the guards talking about the desegregation campaign and immediately went back to the black dorm, where the leaders of the campaign were, to report who was coming and what they were planning. The guards noticed this and quickly fired me from my front office job.

Then I was assigned a job in the jail's farm, a beet field that needed weeding and tending. The true nature of the system we live under became clear to me one day while I was weeding the beet field. I looked up from the valley floor that the jail occupied to the top of the hills that surround it. These hills were covered with track homes looking down on the jail grounds. It was inconceivable to me that anyone could live comfortably within sight of this jail. And yet they did. I realized then that they actually supported our brutal justice system. How I missed this fact until then I can not really say. But it struck me hard in that beet field, cementing my identity as part of the outsiders of our world.

The farm job lasted maybe a day until I was again transferred to a new job. This time my job was at the sewer treatment plant that served the jail. My first day on that job was a shocker. I was given rubber boots and a shovel and ordered to jump down into the sledge pond and shovel the shit into buckets. My next shower was three days away so I was naturally wondering how this was going to work. Fortunately I did not have to wait long to find out because I went to a meeting set up by the demonstrators with the Sheriff to discuss this desegregation plan where I stood up and called the sheriff a liar. Walking out of that meeting, I was immediately busted and sent to solitary wing on the sixth floor of the jail where I was to spend the remainder of my time in jail.

The sixth floor solitary wing was divided into two sections about two thirds of the way down the hall with a wall of bars with a door in it. There were cells lining each side of a long hallway the length of the wing. The far section behind the wall of bars had solid steel doors on each cell. The rest of the wing had regular cell doors with bars. At the entrance to the wing on the right side of the entrance door was a TV hung from the ceiling. They put me in the cell behind the TV. The TV went on in the morning and stayed on all day with the volume cranked all the way up. The inmates would sit on the floor watching it or just glance at it as they walked up and down the corridor all day long in a long circular line. I was locked in my cell for six days before I was allowed to join the circle of men pacing up and down the hallway.

It was a relief at first when they locked me in. I had been in the jail four weeks going from a pampered front office job with a clean ironed shirt everyday, to the white dorm, the black dorm, the beet field, the sewer plant, and then solitary confinement. The cliques of prisoners and demonstrators were vying with each other for everything from desegregating the jail, to beds, cigarettes, special foods, commissary money, telephone calls, and clothing. But as I calmed down a little, the sound of the TV overwhelmed my new isolated space. I couldn't see the screen. I could just hear the stupid shows and the ads, over and over. I had to give those guards credit for picking the exact place that would punish me the most.

I was in this isolation cell when the "riot" broke out. Someone in the black dorm set his mattress on fire which started a huge commotion. It was the time of the 1960's urban riots so the guards freaked out. The whole jail was locked down. The highway patrol was called in along with reinforcements from the sheriff's department. The cops in riot gear quickly occupied the dorm and rounded up a few inmates who they could blame things on. They did not grab the guy who started the fire. Instead, they grabbed the young black supporters of the desegregation plan.

They lined the chosen inmates up in the rotunda outside the dorms and escorted them up to the sixth floor and down the tier to the cells with the solid doors. As they marched the prisoners in a line past my cell door behind the TV, the guard at the end of the line was holding his billy club in both hands, one hand at each end of the club held horizontally. He was pushing the last inmate ahead of him with short brutal motions of his club into the inmates back. The inmate was a young black man in jail for car theft. As he passed my cell door, he spun around and shouted, "I'm going. I'm going. Stop pushing me." The guard then let go of his club with one hand, raised the club with his other hand and smashed this kid in the head. The kid fell to the floor spinning like a top, blood spewing out as he spun. His blood flew through my cell bars and splattered my clothes at about knee high as I stood there watching. The guards then dragged this unconscious kid down the hall leaving a trail of blood on the floor and threw him into one of the isolation cells. I sat down on my bunk, stunned, looking at the blood on my pants in horror. They didn't come back to check on the injured inmate for 12 hours.

When the cops finally walked out of the 6th floor tier, I breathed a sigh of relief that they were not going to come into my cell and teach me a lesson too. They didn't. I will never forget the guard who hit that kid. He was a curly haired bodybuilder type with biceps that filled up his tight short sleeve uniform shirt. Shortly after I got out of jail, my father took me and the family out to dinner to celebrate. As we sat in the House of Prime Rib on Van Ness Ave in San Francisco, this same muscle bound cop walked into the restaurant and sat down at a nearby table. I got up and fled the restaurant with my family immediately.

The rest of my time in the isolation wing of the jail taught me a few more things about the reality of life in our society. Control and domination are the essence of the punishment system, even above violence. The jail served to let inmates know just how powerless they were in our society. Everything was controlled by the cops. Light and dark was controlled depending on when they turned your cell lights off and on. Heat and cold by the blankets they gave you, or took away. Food by what they served off the kitchen wagon that brought the meals to the inmates. At one point I needed to cut my toe nails. Walking in the circle of inmates I asked someone how I could get nail clippers to cut them. Ask the trustee, he said.

That is how I met Pineapple, a Hawaiian inmate who occupied the cell directly across from me (in front of the TV), the trustee's cell. He loaned me a set of clippers. Pineapple was a short powerfully built brown skinned curly haired guy serving a year in county jail on a deal his lawyer made with the courts designed basically to keep him out of San Quentin. He stayed to himself most of the time. If he ever did have to intervene on the tier, he did so with both the authority of his own strength and his position as a trustee of the power structure in the jail.

I noticed that when the food cart went through the tier at meal times, the server would occasionally reach down under the top shelf of the cart and take out something wrapped in paper that looked an awful lot like a hamburger and handed it through the bars to a prisoner. I asked Pineapple how I could get one. He told me I had to give the server two packs of cigarettes and he would bring it the next day. I guessed it was one pack for the server and another for the cook. So the next day, I gathered up two packs of Pall Malls from the commissary and waited for lunch time. I handed the two packs to the server and ordered a hamburger. He took the cigarettes with a grunt and moved on.

Lunch was two pieces of white bread with a slice of baloney in it. I lost ten pounds on that diet and was desperate for some real food. Even though there was general atmosphere of fear surrounding that kind of behavior, there were many other surreptitious pathways for just about everything, from food to clothes and god knows what else.

One day, an old man was brought into the sixth floor and put in one of the cells across from me. He was really drunk and passive about everything. He was skinny as he could be, just a bag of bones really, gray haired with wide eyes staring out desperately from his wrinkled face. Once he was deposited on his bunk, the guard made him take off his wooden leg and hand it to him. From then on the prisoner would have to drag himself around, hop to the toilet on one leg and sit on the floor. He had the DT's and shook uncontrollably for the first couple of days after he arrived. A few days later, as the inmates walked up and down the hallway, one inmate, a big tattooed tough guy smoking a cigarette, passed by this sad old man sitting on the floor with one leg missing. He flicked his cigarette butt into the old guy's face and let out a very ugly laugh. Pineapple was the only one to speak up. "What the fuck is wrong with you?" he shouted as the thug's laugh died away. Other inmates helped the guy now and then during his ten day dry out. And then he was gone.

Stop the Draft Week

The trauma of being jailed for civil rights civil disobedience, it turned out, was good preparation for resisting the draft and refusing to fight in the war in Vietnam. I knew that county jail time was harder than state or federal prison time because of the lack of programs available to prisoners in the county jails compared to state prisons. I could only imagine what a military prison was like. If I had to go to prison, it would be the state prison, not the military prison. But whatever happened, I was determined not to go into the armed services.

Between October, 1966, when I got out of jail, and September, 1967, I continued to live with my wife in Berkeley doing odd jobs. In spite of the great uncertainty hanging over me, I applied to and was accepted into graduate school at the University of Wisconsin, Madison, in history. Within a month of arriving in Madison, I received another scary brown envelope containing my draft notice. "Greetings" it started out. I flew back to Oakland in October, 1967, the week that large militant "Stop the Draft" demonstrations in front of the Oakland Draft Induction Center were taking place. I was supposed to board a bus in Menlo Park where my draft board was located that would take me to the Induction Center in Oakland. My father retained a lawyer, Norm Leonard, who filed a last minute appeal two days before my order to report and, like some kind of miracle, my order to report was postponed again. Instead of boarding that bus and refusing the draft, I joined the demonstrators on the sidewalks in front of the Induction center. Then the next day, flew back to graduate school in Wisconsin.

Fading Out of Academia

When I got back to school, my engagement in discussions with academics about the world had changed. I was in limbo waiting for the next brown envelope after the postponement of my induction. Sitting in classrooms now felt like a repeat of my distracted state when I joined the civil rights movement in Berkeley some years earlier with my radical background invisible to the world. Searching for the truth in academia meant less and less for me. My memory of the green walls of the jail was slowly closing in on me as we all talked about lofty subjects like the profitability of slavery in pre Civil War America. Ha!

Still without career goals, I continued to hope that my Marxist worldview could stand up to PhD level scrutiny, which it did. Pursuing this idea became my day job. My academic work was sandwiched between real jobs painting and repairing student housing as I worked my way through graduate school. I sat in class with one of the sons of Julius and Ethel Rosenberg (the executed "atomic spies") whose background was even more invisible than mine and was not discussed at all.

In my side jobs I discovered new things about living in a frozen climate with basements built below the freeze line and tornadoes hiding in the clouds. Meanwhile, National Guard troops occupied the Madison campus as it convulsed with anti Vietnam war demonstrations. A bomb went off in a research building on campus, killing a graduate student. I became an open Communist and got called a Stalinist. Once again, Communist Party radicals were providing local community connections for student radicals, draft counselors, and demonstrations against the war in Vietnam.

When my wife became pregnant with our first child, I immediately informed the draft board. They quickly sent me a III-A deferment. Surprised and relieved, that ended my struggle to stay out of the Vietnam war. When the draft stopped coming after me in 1969, all the air went out of my sails. I quit the party wondering what the future held. The day I quit the party, Bob Starobin, my friend and history teacher in Madison, knocked on my front door unannounced. I opened it and he said, "Welcome to the human race." I was more confused than ever. A few years later, Bob committed suicide.

By the time I returned to California in 1972, I was still following the default assumption in the History Department that I would become a teacher and spend my time teaching and researching in dark archives, writing academic articles for professional journals I detested. I worked as a college professor for three years at St. Mary's College in Moraga, California. In 1978, I turned in my PhD dissertation, quit teaching and went to work in the building trades as a carpenter. I mailed off the final draft of the dissertation dressed in jeans, boots and a work shirt on my way to a job in a van filled with tools, most of which came from my father's garage.

Leaving the Academic World

Leaving the academic world was a tremendous relief. It allowed me to turn my full attention to more earthly matters. My attraction to carpentry focused me on wood. Trees held me in their power. I was fascinated by them. I loved the forests which my father had been photographing since I was a boy. But as a city boy, the idea of becoming a forester, or a camper, or a logger did not interest me. What interested me was constructing the means of survival out of the natural world around me with my own hands. I had a direct self interest in that. First, becoming a carpenter was a way to actually survive in the world without a security check and without any intellectual baloney. Second, it gave me job skills I could make a living with. When I told people in those years that I taught history, the most frequent response I got was "oh, I hate history." In contrast, when I told them I was a carpenter, the most frequent response I got was, "May I have your card?"

My environmental awareness grew as I became aware of the real world around me. I was caught between loving the forests and making a living by cutting them down. In the 1970's, it was not clear to me yet that cutting down the forests was destroying the balance of nature and leading us to disaster. It was just the world I lived in and needed to find a way to survive. That is blindness in action.

Water led me to understand my contradictory role even better. Building and repairing houses is all about water. When I first started working in house repair, I saw the impact of water on houses. I began to see how roof water soaked the foundations of houses causing settlement and cracks that let water into the walls and crawl spaces causing rot and other kinds of structural decay. I noticed downspouts carrying roof water to the ground, right at the foundation. Since heavy things sink in the mud, diverting roof water away from the house was obviously the thing to do.

Then, I asked myself what happened to the roof water when it was drained away from the foundations to the street, or off the lot? Where did it go? What happened when it got to the creek? Where were the creeks and what were their names? Nameless creeks were mostly underground in culverts draining to unknown rivers. Rain water drained across hardscapes that make up most of the surfaces in a city. Downpours drained water away quickly in floods because the ground was covered with concrete roads, patios, driveways and house roofing. The earth couldn't absorb the water. I worked for a short time with a paving company putting down sidewalks and parking lots and experienced how extensive these hardscapes were. I found some solace in the idea that I was working with the natural world to help create survival for people and myself. But gradually I saw that this very process was compounding the problem and it was only getting worse as urban society grew and grew.

How did these real problems relate to my Marxism? I was witnessing the class struggle sinking into the fat recliner chairs in front of ever larger TVs in the suburban living rooms of our ever expanding cities. Workers were not rising up against the destruction of the planet. No, oil workers were against solar power. Miners wanted jobs excavating mountain tops and filling up creeks to get at the coal. Loggers fought for their jobs, clear cutting the forests. And I gladly bought the lumber for my jobs. Only a few isolated scientists, sports people, environmentalists, and native tribes were speaking up about the Earth. Western mainstream cultures supported the supremacy of private property with its political warfare economy and its brutal justice system. There seemed to be no escape from a society in which the blind were leading the blind.

Part 2: The Circle of the People

5: Environmental Awareness

At the same time that I was running construction crews, pounding nails and pouring concrete, I began to wonder again about the indigenous spiritual world outside the modern urban framework that had shaped me. I had walled off the spiritual world from my daily life over the years, viewing it as a remnant of the past irrelevant to the present modern world. When I read Russell Means' 1980 speech that indicted us for despiritualizing nature, I thought back to the time when I first became aware of the natural world in high school. My father and stepmother, Alice Richards, sent my brother and me off to a boarding school near Sedona, Arizona where I found myself living outside a city for the first time. I was 15 years old, in the tenth grade.

Verde Valley School

I attended Verde Valley School (VVS) from 1958 to 1961. Verde Valley was completely different from the urban schools of Oakland I had attended up to that time. Instead of large crowded under-funded multi racial institutions, Verde Valley had 120 students in total (mostly white) with class sizes of 10 at the most. The student body included boys and girls living and studying in a small cluster of buildings out in the middle of a gently sloping alluvial plain situated below fantastical red rock formations looming up all around us. I could walk out of the dormitory into a dry creek bed (called washes) and within minutes be sitting alone with the stars shining brightly in the sky. No cars rushing by. No sirens sounding in the distance. No street lights obscuring the heavens. Of course, I was wonderfully blind to this miraculous natural setting being submerged in normal teenage pouting and hormonal confusion. It was a great place to smoke a cigarette in secret and find friends among other students out there sneaking around in the dark. I was unaware of how the place, with its magical red rocks, had prepared me for the comparative religion courses taught by a remarkable man named Joseph Epes Brown.

Joe Brown

I had always approached religion under the heading of "opium of the people." This reticence laid quietly in the back of my mind as I attended his classes. Joe was the author of *The Sacred Pipe: The Seven Rites of the Oglala Sioux.* His book was based on his interview with Black Elk, a Sioux holy man, in 1947. Joe Brown was a quiet and charming man who did not engage my contrary nature. His teachings and example as a man turned on a light for me that shined brighter as the years passed.

The stigma of my communist family had followed me to the school. My father had been required to bring my brother and me to the school in the summer of

1958 for interviews before we were admitted. I learned later the interviews were ordered because my father had been called before the House UnAmerican Activities Committee (HUAC) as a communist. When they found that we boys didn't have horns or red tails, they let us in. Once in classes there, my history teacher lectured me about Russia for reasons I did not appreciate. He brought out my rebellious nature and evoked my quick fight-back as I rejected every power structure around me, including Verde Valley School's.

Joe Brown was different. He invited elders from the nearby Hopi, Zuni, and Navajo reservations to speak to our classes and school assemblies. These holy men did not evoke any fight back in me. Instead, they evoked shame that I was so ignorant of their ways. They introduced me to an alternative way of life, something I had never seen before. My first glimpse came with a story they told about how Navajo students would not raise their hands in class even though they knew the answers. Instead they remained silent in order not to shame anyone who did not know the answer. As a student in classrooms since I was 5 years old, I understood this shame completely. The idea that the whole class would stand in solidarity with the one who did not know had a great appeal to me. No winners and losers. That was it for me. It was a door into a mindset outside western civilization.

Joe Brown's influence on me deepened even more because of horses. VVS kept a stable of horses for students and staff. Some of the richer students actually brought their horses with them to the school. Having never been around horses, I checked them out and found myself very interested in riding. Soon I was mucking out stalls, maintaining saddles and bridles, and throwing around bales of hay and buckets of oats.

Joe owned a horse and spent time at the stables after his duties teaching comparative religions. He took some of us student riders on overnight trips in the countryside around Sedona. His own horse, Patrushka, was a gray, tall, long legged Arabian thoroughbred he had trained in the manner he learned from the Sioux. They did not break horses by getting on and letting them buck until they were broken. He made friends with Patrushka, earning her trust by rubbing her down with gentle hands, and feeding her. Only he and his wife, Elenita, could ride that horse. Patrushka was frisky and very different from the other "broken" horses. Joe would ride her without a bridle, using his legs to turn her left or right, or go fast or slow. Joe laughed out loud as the horse alternatively obeyed and disobeyed his commands. It scared me when I saw him do that. I wondered how he would ever get off without being injured. Since I did not know horses, I feared they would seek revenge by kicking or biting, or that they would run away. But he did trust Patrushka and always managed to get off safely. My cultural view of nature as hostile and alien contrasted deeply with Joe's trust and unity with nature and his horse.

On our camping trips, we hobbled the horses at night with leg cuffs that were supposed to keep them from running very far off. Except Patrushka. Joe would not allow it. In the morning, we awoke to find the horses were gone. We had to follow their tracks on foot as Patrushka had led all the hobbled horses miles away. Joe found this very amusing. I did not. Now I understand it better. Over the years I have come to realize the great impact those horseback outings had on me. I was witnessing the kind of relations that indigenous people had with nature. We found the horses and led them back to our camp for the ride back to the school. Joe hopped on Patrushka without a saddle or bridle and led the way.

Joe's Indian guests' talks made a big impression on me, too, introducing me to tribal ideas of the unity of all life and their respect for nature and all their relations among the plant and animal world. I had never heard anyone say these things, so far beyond the confines of my radical Oakland childhood. The words of these holy men left me in awe, although I never talked about it then nor admitted it even to myself.

Like all school children, I had been subjected to endless talking over the years in school during which I developed escape spaces in my mind in order to get through it. But these quiet old men's words pierced the walls of my boredom and resistance, leaving permanent impressions that grew and grew over the years. Their relatives among the animal world? How had I missed this? The only animals in my world had been our dogs I witnessed dying under the wheels of passing cars and from poison thrown over our fence designed to stop their barking. Lights came on in my head. Here suddenly was a culture that validated my deepest feelings and revealed the reality of our ways.

Looking back on it, I can see now that my rebellious Marxist tendencies co-existed with these indigenous ways like two separate boats floating in a lake. My radicalism left me facing in one direction, while the new insights gained through Joe Brown's teachings tagged along separately from my fundamental orientation. Indigenous respect for nature was a good idea, but it did not inform or transform the Marxist rebellion then brewing in my teenage self.

These two worlds surfaced on their own in a poem I wrote for an English class. Writing a poem was a challenging assignment for me. I had to recite it to the class. I had never done anything like that before. I wrote the poem one day as I was laying on my stomach out in the sun on a flagstone patio near the recreation room for the dorm I lived in. Ants were crawling in a line across the patio. An idea struck me and I wrote this poem:

> *You know,*
> *bees are pretty basic*
> *must have brains*
> *as big as a pin point.*
>
> *They all work together*
> *some get food*
> *and some make housing*
> *all for one and*
> *one for all*
>
> *You know,*
> *someone ought to tell them*
> *that's socialism*

I submitted the poem and read it to the class, where it was received with silence. Some days later, I was summoned to report to the dean of students office. The dean was a retired Air Force colonel. I entered the room and sat down. Sitting next to the dean was the English teacher and her husband, the school's history teacher.

The history teacher and I had clashed since the very first day of school. On that day, I met him sitting with several other new students at the table in the dining hall. There were plates set out with a slice of white bread on each plate. I took a bite of the white bread. This guy, who was also the faculty in charge of my dorm, instructed me, "At Verde Valley, we break our bread," he said. I had no idea that breaking up your slice of bread was even something that people did. I was so upset by this humiliation, that I proceeded to break the piece of bread into tiny bits, throwing them each dramatically onto the plate in front of me. In history classes, he would lecture us on the history of Russia, adding lines like, "Things weren't so great in Russia, Richards."

Now in the colonel's office, he and his wife sat grim faced. They accused me of plagiarizing the poem. I was shocked. I almost laughed out loud. That had to be the biggest compliment I had ever received! They must have thought that the poem was too good for the likes of me to have written. I suppressed a smile and promised I would produce my notes to show that I had written it. The poem had popped out of my head in one piece that day on the flagstone patio so I didn't really have any notes beside the page I wrote it on. I submitted my notes and never heard another word, not even an apology. My sense of the natural world expressed in this simple poem had landed me in trouble. Facing the wall of disbelief and disapproval from the colonel and the teachers left me with lasting images of my place in the world. It was no wonder that I found the teachings of Joe Brown so appealing.

Intermountain School for Indians

Verde Valley School took all the students on innovative trips to the southwest Indian reservations each year. Students could sign up for trips to Canyon DeChelly to visit archaeological sites, or stay with families in hogans out in the reservation somewhere, or take a trip to Gallup New Mexico to visit museums. One year, 1960 if I remember correctly, I signed up for the trip to the Inter-Mountain School for Indians in Brigham City, Utah. We traveled there in the back of a green flat bed truck with a big box body and a cab overhang. There were windows on both sides and mats on the floor. The school had a fleet of these trucks for the trips. We were dropped off to spend 5 days living in the dormitory and going to classes with the Indian students. I don't remember why I signed up for such a trip. Maybe just because I had never been to Utah before. It certainly was not a carefully thought out choice. But the experience, which was not a good one, was a lasting one.

The Indian students greeted us in sullen silence with icy stares. The boys were all nicely dressed with crew cuts. The chilly silences and sterile surroundings left me in dread of each day as we ventured out from our dormitory beds to attend academic classes, classes in car mechanics, and home economics. I wondered why were we here? Was it to show what a good job the US government was doing to help the Indians? All the floors in the building were sparkling clean and waxed. The classrooms were modern and shining. The car mechanics classes had up to date tools and engine blocks arrayed neatly for students to dissect. The home economics classes were full of sinks and stoves and work tables. Or were there some other reasons? What would Joe Brown's holy men have thought of it? I felt the horror below the hypnotizing impact of all the sparkling things around everywhere.

When the school truck finally showed up five days later to take us back, we all jumped for joy. As we drove off, one student pulled down his pants and "mooned" the school with his bare ass pressed up against the truck window. We all roared with laughter.

Over the years that followed I learned about the role of these schools in trying to destroy the Indian student's cultures through forced separations from their families and outlawing of their language. They were supposed to learn trades like mechanics or cooking to help them fit into the US dominant white world. They didn't like that one bit and it showed. At the time, we looked on these Indian students with pity but little sympathy. In a way, we were in the same boat as they were, living in boarding schools away from our families. I was unaware that they were prisoners of the boarding school whereas we were attending VVS voluntarily and in luxury. We were just glad we were not them. When we got back to the campus in Sedona, no explanations or historical insights about such a place were offered to us.

Realizing later how deeply hurtful and destructive these schools were, I came to understand what I had seen. When I studied World War II, I came across photos of the concentration camps with prisoners staring through barbed wire fences with those same looks on their faces. A sadness rose in me from something I still cannot name.

These high school experiences with Joe Brown, horses, and Indian holy men had planted a seed that disturbed the western values inside me. Years and decades passed during which I was submerged in the concrete world of cities and the compelling social web of my peers and institutions like Verde Valley School, UC Berkeley, the University of Wisconsin, Madison, the San Francisco County Jail, and the Communist Party. My rebellious nature got a full workout in those years with all the 1960's demonstrations, police occupations of campuses, and frequent tear gas attacks. But living as the radical in the room, the loser in the fight for justice and peace, I was still blind to the spiritual world around me.

New Directions: Visiting the USSR

My search for socialist alternatives to war and racism began in earnest in the summer after I graduated from Verde Valley school. I returned home to Oakland where my whole world was about to drop out from under me. The tranquil life among the red rocks of Arizona gave way to the Oakland streets where I moved in temporarily with my mother, step father, and sister. My brother had graduated from VVS the year before and much to everyone's surprise, joined the Navy and went off to basic training somewhere.

Just as I settled in alone without my brother now in our Oakland family home, my father asked me if I wanted to accompany him and my stepmother, Alice, on a film making trip to the USSR to help him carry his equipment and batteries. I accepted gladly and off we went on my first airplane ride to Europe and the Soviet Union to make a film about women and children in a socialist society. I was already aware of socialism and admired Russia like a child admired his parent's favorite things. When we arrived in Moscow, we were greeted by a group of Soviet women from the Soviet Women's Committee who helped us set up our itinerary, provided us with translators, and helped with all the paperwork.

I wouldn't say that my father had to drag me along, but almost. I reverted back to the passive hormone obsessed teen missing my friends, bored with the adult world, embarrassed by pregnant women, babies and other people's apartments, schools, factories that we visited. We stayed in a big hotel in Moscow with Stalinesque architecture, big empty lobbies, and sparsely filled restaurants that took hours and hours to get meals in. All the waiters wore white aprons or smocks and came to the table only after long absences between courses of the meal. When we finally went up to our rooms and settled down for the night, I was still full of energy but glad to be alone without anything to do or any heavy equipment to marshal around. I sat in my room looking out the window onto the dimly lit Moscow streets wondering what I could do. One night, I walked out the front door of the hotel alone and wandered through the dark night with no destination in mind.

Coming from Oakland, I was accustomed to being careful at night. I looked closely at the buildings and the few people also walking around looking for the tell tale signs of danger. I was a little jittery at first and just walked down the sidewalks until I was out of sight of the hotel. I couldn't read the Russian words on street signs so I just had to pick out buildings and trees so I could find my way back.

Soon I started to relax because I didn't find any signs of danger. As a matter of fact, just the opposite. I came across a small kiosk on the sidewalk selling vodka. Being a big tall kid, I had no trouble looking 18, their drinking age. Not that it mattered to the kiosk guy. So I ordered vodka. They served it in these big shot glasses. I had observed the Russian way of drinking back in the hotel restaurant. You slugged it back in one big gulp. So that's what I did. The kiosk seller smiled broadly with approval as I drank it down. Then I walked on marveling at the fact that I felt safe on the streets at night. There were no gangs lurking in the darkness. There were no old loud cars slowly rumbling down the street full of scary people I could not see. No homeless, destitute people sleeping in dark corners. I was experiencing something new. I had just expanded my world into a new space where I wandered at night without fear.

As Russian as everything was, it was still socialism I was wandering in without fear, reinforcing my young socialist convictions with another lasting experience.

You Can't Go Home Again

Returning from the Soviet Union in late August, 1961, we drove from the airport to my father's Atherton home and put all the filming equipment away. I jumped into my '57 Chevy that my father had given me when he bought his Oldsmobile station wagon in 1960, and drove "home" to Oakland. I was full of anticipation moving back to my old stomping grounds I had been missing ever since going to Verde Valley three years earlier. I decided to start my freshman year living at home since the drive from Oakland to Berkeley is only a few minutes.

It was a strange time for me as a 17 year old teenager returning to my childhood home and neighborhood on the way to a new life away at college. For the first month I commuted to Berkeley for my classes and back to Oakland at night. I had lost contact almost completely with my old friends and neighbors which became clear to me one day when I was getting into the Chevy at the curb in front of my house. Two young black kids, 7 or 8 years old, came walking around the corner across the street, looked at me, laughing, and called out "Hippy!" I automatically looked down at what I was wearing, standing there with my crew cut hair, my button down short sleeve shirt, khakis and brown loafers. Hippy? My home on the corner of 23rd Ave and East 19th Street was in a poor mixed race (white, black, Mexican, Chinese) neighborhood.

Calling me a hippy was different than being called a redneck. The cultural revolution of the 1960's was splitting me into pieces. Growing up as a white boy in Oakland had occasionally put me into confrontations with black kids strictly on racial lines. My black friends, who knew my interracial family, often kept me safe. Now, grown to my full six foot one inch height and out of touch with the kids in the neighborhood, me and my crew cut were the image of the dominant society. It was not my clothes they were deriding. Instead they were associating me with the new long haired rock and roll rebellion that was making the straight world so outraged. As rock and roll swept the country, moving from Elvis Presley to the longish haired Beetles, I longed for some way to distinguish myself from the mainstream without growing my hair long. What was I going to say to these boys? "I am not a Hippy?" So I swallowed the insult and went off to college.

Once back home in the Bay Area, I took refuge in my leftist political perspective against the rising tide of cultural alienation that infected my generation. Not only that, I also took refuge in black culture that had been part of my upbringing since I was two years old. I may have loved Elvis Presley, the Beatles and Mose Allison, but I also loved Jimmy Reed, Ella Fitzgerald, Duke Ellington, Muddy Waters, John Lee Hooker, and BB King. My family included blacks which left me identifying myself with humanism over everything else.

My invisible black roots and my radical political bent left me in limbo both politically and culturally. The slogans of the time echoed in my head. "Kill a commie for Christ!", "Better dead than red," "Nigger Lover," combined with the epithets hurled at me at school like "Your mommy is a commie!" At the same time, I realized that if I were walking down the street, black people would never greet me with the nod of recognition that was always there for other blacks passing by. The 1960's hippy alienation was not yet for me.

I studied history, taking courses in US and European history, logic and political science. The real world cast a shadow over the student movement as we joined the nationwide protests against racial segregation and the war in Vietnam. We marched to the Oakland Army Base to urge soldiers not to go to war. By the time the Free Speech movement erupted in 1964, I had already been arrested and convicted three times in trials in the San Francisco courts. I wished them luck but did not follow the students into Sproul Hall to confront University leaders trying to squash the rebellion. I was busy marching in ever larger and longer peace mobilizations against the war in Vietnam down Market Street in San Francisco. And throughout these turbulent years, my father showed up with his cameras filming the protests that underlay the cultural and political upheavals all around us. (See Chapter 15: Growing Doubts for more.)

Immediately after graduating in the winter of 1966, the draft came after me. My student deferment ended and I was ordered to report for my pre-induction physical. My struggle against the draft dominated my life for three years from 1966 to 1969. After I escaped the draft, cultural alienation caught up with me in a whole new way. I had always seen myself and other rebels as trying to change the narrative. But when the draft released me, the dialog and the narrative lost their importance for me. I was free to dream. The arrival of my first born child had ended my struggle against the Selective Service Draft Board with a III-A classification. In 1966, I felt like a hunted animal when I received my order to report for induction on the first day in jail serving my sentence for the civil rights sit-ins two years earlier. In 1970, no longer fearing jail or induction into our imperialist army, I was cut loose from the 1960's rebellions that had consumed me for so many years.

6: Turn On, Tune In, and Drop Out

Drifting through my thirties in the 1970's led me directly to Timothy Leary's advice to "Turn on, tune in, and drop out." I was late to the party because I had always feared dropping acid, believing it threatened to knock the pillars out from under my known world. When I arrived in the limbo of the years after the draft stopped chasing me, I really no longer knew my world. So why not knock down those pillars? I thought maybe those pillars needed to be knocked down. It was a moment when I felt that uncertainty was all I had. My world was dissolving.

Dropping Acid

I was worried and cautious about taking acid. A friend agreed to be my "guide", supplied me with the hits and a place in the country where I could experience it. Many years later I found out that this "friend" had been flown across the country to Washington, DC, twice by the CIA during the years we were all involved in the protests against the draft and racism. This discovery dovetailed nicely with the documented fact of that agency's involvement in bringing acid to the dissidents of the time. As Steven Kinser said in his 2020 interview with Dave Davies on NPR about the CIA's 10 year long MKUltra experiments with LSD,

> *it's a tremendous irony that the drug that the CIA hoped would be its key to controlling humanity actually wound up fueling a generational rebellion that was dedicated to destroying everything that the CIA held dear and defended.*[3]

I finally took my first magical mystery tour one spring day in Mendocino county north of San Francisco on a forested piece of fenced in property I had never visited before nor since. The trees were a mix of oak and pine. The grass was green. As the acid came on, waves of energy and trembling pulsed up and down my body. I thought I might explode as I ran exuberantly back and forth across a grassy green field. We were on a hillside overlooking a county road. At times, I sat in the grass quietly amazed at the transformation of the ordinary world into an electromagnetic light show. Cars whizzed by occasionally hissing through the air like bullets. I sat on the ground touching it with my outstretched hand, looking at the grass and dirt in a completely different way. All the living things glowed with a metallic light I had never seen before. The magic of the world's spiritual nature entered my body and mind.

At first I thought, oh yes, I want to live in this world forever. For two or three days, the electromagnetic lights kept shining. But they soon faded and the ordinary shape of things returned. I tried acid a couple more times, each time with less impact. Depression followed each trip. Then I was back to work, teaching history. The pull of the real world would not go away. My son was a toddler now and the rent was due. If I kept dropping acid, I feared I would ruin my life. So I put my head down and plowed ahead the best I could.

Smoking weed became an everyday thing that went on for decades after. My first hit on a marijuana joint happened when I was 11 years old in Oakland when it was illegal. I didn't smoke it much after that until years later. Then, in 1972, as my crisis orientation dissolved, so did my marriage. My daughter was born in 1972 just when my pot smoking was maxing out and my personal disintegration was at its height. My marriage was in trouble as the world I had known slipped away from me, leaving me floating in uncertainty. I seemed to be sleep walking into my future.

I realized that, with my divorce, I was traveling in my father's footsteps. I was the second generation to go through something like this. My father and mother had also divorced after 10 years of marriage with two children, one four years old and the other two years old. Now my children were those same ages, as Susan and I separated and divorced after 10 years of marriage. I couldn't believe it was happening and I couldn't change anything. Was it fate? Karma? Whatever it was, it was otherworldly.

As my initial joy from the acid trip faded into the background, smoking weed became my way to hang on to it. But before long, staying high all the time created a wall between my life and the reality around me. That was the idea, actually, but it lost its appeal as my awareness turned elsewhere, as the natural world loomed larger and larger in my mind and life.

Ram Dass

Very soon after the acid trip, I found Ram Dass, aka Richard Alpert, a sidekick of Timothy Leary at Harvard where they both experimented with LSD in research programs. Ram Dass, a professor of psychology, had been fired from Harvard, like Leary, and then gone to India in 1967. He found a guru, and shortly afterwards, put out his wonderful book *Be Here Now*. I found this book in the form of an audio recording of Ram Dass reading the whole book. I sank into the euphoria of his voice and listened to it over and over. I loved his mantra, "Don't worry about the future, just be here now." I repeated it to myself and others endlessly in those years.

Ram Dass told the story of giving his Indian guru some acid to see what he thought of it. To his surprise it did nothing to his guru at all. Then he recounted how he realized that acid, like tobacco or weed, only worked to put up a smoke screen between one's consciousness and reality. It worked because it created the illusion of separateness. As my environmental awareness grew, I could see that I was part of the earth, and that separateness was what I was running from. That insight stuck in my mind until I finally decided I did not need the dope anymore.

Quitting dope was not some heroic act of self control on my part. It came to me naturally, like the old ditty "I love to bang my head on the wall because it feels so good when I stop." My brief encounter with cocaine taught me another lesson about dope. With cocaine, it was obvious that its role was to make you numb. And why, I asked myself, was that so appealing to so many, including myself? When one's life is full of pain, numbing up seems like a great improvement. But like with acid, there was always the problem of coming down. The pain returned and its impact grew. It was a vicious cycle that was not only destructive psychologically, but in every other way. It cost a lot of money and ruined relationships. It cost me all of that until, thanks to Ram Dass, I saw it for what it was and turned away from it.

When the imperialist state took its foot off my neck, a huge vacuum arose inside me. Starobin had been right. I had joined the human race in more ways than I cared to admit. No longer knowing myself, I fell out of the world of resistance and struggle into this new reality like a man stumbling in the dark. Soon, I was divorced, leaving two small children with their mother and wandering brokenhearted, more lost than ever. I found a small apartment in Oakland near Lake Merritt and continued teaching in spite of my growing dissatisfaction with the life of a professor. My world shattered and fell away piece by piece as I experienced each day filled with anxiety rising up inside me.

My environmental awareness did not spring up brand new in the void created by the collapse of my world in the early 1970's. As I recovered from my divorce, the acid trip, and my flight from academia, a new focus arose for me. My old agenda had been wiped clean. Now, I began to understand my place in the world differently as I focused on the simpler things in front of me. Things like dirt, wood, water, air, gas, and the poisons constantly accompanying my every move. I was not a scientist in a lab looking at some experiment in test tubes. I had broken out of the narrow possibilities of the academic profession and landed with two feet squarely on the ground. I was keenly aware of the human complexity surrounding my place on the Earth.

While all the crises that had dominated my life for so many years were now behind me, their impact remained. I was like a person with post traumatic stress syndrome, upset and bracing myself for catastrophe all the time. I wanted to stop looking over my shoulder, bracing myself for trouble. I wanted to stop standing on a cliff's edge constantly ready to jump. The only moments of relief I could find were the creative times building and repairing things. I gravitated to those moments like a man clinging to a life raft. When I met Nina Serrano, a creative poetic woman, my creative world expanded another step. Soon we were living together and 12 years later we married. That was 4 decades ago.

It was in this transitional state of mind that I began to dig deeper into the environmental world I was now immersed in. All the years in academia had not disappeared from my head, however. Now the world view that resulted from years of studying the economic history of the west became the filter through which I observed my new situation.

7: The Circle of the People

In my brief sojourn as a history professor at St. Mary's College in Moraga, California (1972-75), I found myself drawn to native American history through the teachings of Black Elk who Joe Brown wrote about in his book *The Sacred Pipe: Black Elk's Account of the Seven Rites of the Oglala Sioux*. Black Elk was a Sioux holy man who lived from 1863 to 1950. He articulated the concept of the circle of the people in his interviews with two western writers, John Neihardt and Joseph Epes Brown.

> *Everything the Power of the World does is done in a circle. The sky is round, and I have heard that the earth is round like a ball, and so are all the stars. The wind, in its greatest power, whirls. Birds make their nest in circles, for theirs is the same religion as ours. The sun comes forth and goes down again in a circle. The moon does the same and both are round. Even the seasons form a great circle in their changing, and always come back again to where they were. The life of a man is a circle from childhood to childhood, and so it is in everything where power moves. Our tepees were round like the nests of birds, and these were always set in a circle, the nation's hoop.*[4]

The circle of the people appealed to my socialist core. "From each according to his ability, to each according to his needs." That was the credo underlying my allegiance to Marxism. The circle of the people, however, went beyond the rational socialist credo of the man made world. It included the birds, the sky, the planets, and stars. This made it into an even more radical concept. The circle of the people did not deny the scientific interrelations between human and other forms of life or between us and the celestial reality surrounding us. It simply asserted the truth of the spiritual relationships of all existence. I knew inside that this spiritual reality was happening. But my anti-religious (opium of the people) predisposition still left me silently wondering.

As a builder, I built square spaces, square rooms, square foundations, square walls, windows, doors, etc. Hardly ever circles. Square spatial orientation is what I was born into and what I, and almost everyone else, have lived in my entire life. Going beyond the square to understand the circle is a fundamental reorientation of the mind and body. The square breaks us into separate entities. The circle unites us in one reality. When I first read about the circle of the people, I viewed the idea as part of an old myth, a lost past, now irrelevant to modern life. It appeared to me a remote notion, removed from the possibilities of our lives today. The inertia and immensity of modern urban life blinded me to its meaning. After all, we don't need to change anything if we know that it is impossible. The weight of the present had been propelling my thinking into a false image of the future.

The circle of the people did not fit into the long suffering working class mentality I grew up with. Nor did it fit into the anti-racist civil rights struggles or the anti-imperialist peace movement I had obsessed on for decades. Instead, the idea of the circle of the people lay dormant in my mind. I knew it was real, but like a melancholy dream, it lay separately from the world of fighting for peace and justice within the mainstream.

I found myself outlining Black Elk's vision for my students at St. Mary's College. I assigned the book *Black Elk Speaks* by John Neihardt and painstakingly reviewed how a dream that Black Elk had as a nine year old boy unfolded with black board diagrams and lengthy readings of the text. Seeing the stacks of Neihardt's books in the book store and on the students' desks was deeply satisfying. The blank stares and silences of the students were the big challenges.

I did not see the circle of the people as something to go to war for. The tribes fought for their land and their cultures. The circle of the people was their way to live peacefully. Western minds saw it as paganism and the work of the devil. Unsurprising to me, it was just the opposite. I looked at the bright young faces of my students (not much younger than I was) and realized that I wanted to give them some idea of this cause for peace. I decided to describe Black Elk's dream in full detail in order to make it memorable. They asked me if the dream would be on their test. I sighed and said yes, not really intending to test them at all.

We all labored under the weight of our cultural assumptions about Indians and the land we all lived on. The only thing that might weaken these foundational views, I reasoned, was to help the students understand Black Elk's dream and thereby open their eyes to the Sioux culture out of which it came.

Now, as I sit here writing, I see that Black Elk helped me comprehend Russell Means' indictment of European blindness. My own blindness to the spiritual nature of the Earth began to recede as the lights came on illuminating this new reality. The two separate spaces in my inner reality (the radical fighter and the spiritual being) began to merge.

I left the college curriculum behind, rejecting both the demands of the job and the expectations of the students. The pull of this new spiritual perspective revealed by the dream pulled me away from my job just like the civil rights movement and the war in Vietnam pulled me away from my studies years earlier. What the hell, I thought, here I was giving my students grades that might lead to their being drafted into the war. I handed out grades with no concern for the student's performance. I was definitely unfit for the job.

The story of Black Elk's dream took me into the other world, a story outside my Marxist mindset with its rationalism and Christian Judaic roots. The story in the dream is one thing, outlined below. The dream itself, the idea that such dreams happen, is another. While I could hardly understand it as a young professor, I knew it was something profound that I could not ignore. Here was an old man, Black Elk, in the 1930's, describing a vision he had decades earlier as a nine year old boy that revealed the truth of what was unfolding in his time and mine in the 1970's and what would happen in the decades ahead. Instead of teaching the students the names of the generals and the chiefs in the battle of the

Little Bighorn, I was outlining the dream of a nine year old boy.

8: Black Elk's Dream

Black Elk told his dream to John Neihardt in the 1930s. He began the story by smoking the sacred pipe with Neihardt so that "only good would go between them". The story of the sacred pipe set the stage for the vision within the traditional world view of the Sioux people. Black Elk's story of the sacred pipe's origin starts with two scouts out hunting bison, when, at the top of a hill, a sacred woman appears.

Then one of the scouts, being foolish, had bad thoughts and spoke them; but the other said: "This is a sacred woman; throw all bad thoughts away." When she came still closer, they saw that she wore a fine white buckskin dress, that her hair was very long and that she was young and very beautiful. And she knew their thoughts and said in a voice that was like singing: "You do not know me, but if you want to do as you think, you may come." And the foolish one went; but just as he stood before her, there was a white cloud that came and covered them. And the beautiful young woman came out of the cloud, and when it blew away the foolish man was a skeleton covered with worms.

Then the woman spoke to the one who was not foolish: "You shall go home and tell your people that I am coming and that a big tepee shall be built for me in the center of the nation." And the man, who was very much afraid, went quickly and told the people, who did at once as they were told; and there around the big tepee they waited for the sacred woman. And after a while she came, very beautiful and singing....

And as she sang, there came from her mouth a white cloud that was good to smell. Then she gave something to the chief, and it was a pipe with a bison calf carved on one side to mean the earth that bears and feeds us, and with twelve eagle feathers hanging from the stem to mean the sky and the twelve moons, and these were tied with a grass that never breaks. "Behold!" she said.

"With this you shall multiply and be a good nation. Nothing but good shall come from it. Only the hands of the good shall take care of it and the bad shall not even see it."[5]

The sacred woman lived at the center of the nation. She was not made from Adam's rib, nor did she emerge from the froth foaming up after Greek God Ouranos' genitals were castrated and thrown into the sea. She was the one who gave them the sacred pipe and the good path for the people to follow. At the time I first encountered this sacred woman, I did not realize who I was seeing. The Goddess was making her first appearance.

Black Elk told Neihardt of a time when he was sick and feverish in his parent's tepee. His visionary dream started with two men coming from the clouds. They beckoned him to follow them. They had long spears with lightning flashing from the points. He went with them, no longer in pain, on a little cloud to a world of clouds. The three of them were alone in the middle of a great white plain, with snowy hills and mountains.

The Four Directions

A Bay horse appeared and beckoned "Behold me. My life-history you shall see." The four directions, north, south, east and west, were full of 12 horses in each direction. Black horses where the sun goes down (west). White horses where the great white giant lives (north). Sorrel horses where the sun shines continually (east). Buckskin horses where you are always looking (south). Great sounds of whinnying and nickering accompanied the appearance of a mighty wind with horses without number of all colors whinnying and nickering back at the black, white, sorrel and buckskin horses, now formed into four abreast formations marching forward. The horses without numbers turned into all the animals of the world and disappeared into the four directions. Animals led Black Elk into the dream reminding me how horses had led me into my first experiences with Joe Brown on that camping trip.

Council of Grandfathers

The Bay horse led Black Elk and his two messengers to a council of grandfathers. The clouds changed into a tepee. Its door was a rainbow. Inside six old men ("they looked older than men can ever be") sat in a row. Black Elk went in, standing in front of the six Grandfathers. The oldest spoke, "Your Grandfathers all over the world are having a council, and they have called you here to teach you." Black Elk realized these six were not old men at all, "but the Powers of the World. And the first was the Power of the West; the second, of the North; the third, of the East; the fourth, of the South; the fifth, of the Sky; the sixth, of the Earth."

The grandfathers personified the powers of the world. They were not male gods in the sky creating things. The powers of the world were the natural four legged and winged creatures, and creatures with roots, who coexisted with us and showed us how to live. This was a world view in stark contrast to monotheistic, male dominated views of the conquerors thinking they had dominion over the Earth. Living in harmony with all of nature was the essence of the grandfathers' identity.

One at a time, the Powers of the World talked with Black Elk. The first Grandfather spoke saying that Black Elk would go "to the high center of the earth that you may see; even to the place where the sun continually shines, they shall take you there to understand."

Water is Life

The first grandfather handed him a wooden cup full of water and said, "Take this. It is the power to make live and it is yours." Next he handed him a bow and said, "Take this. It is the power to destroy, and it is yours. Then he pointed to himself and said: 'Look close at him who is your spirit now, for you are his body....'" The Grandfathers showed him the thunder nation, the white geese nation. They gave him the power to heal and the power to awaken "all the beings of the earth with roots and legs and wings." They handed him the peace pipe and said "With this pipe, you shall walk upon the earth, and whatever sickens there you shall make well." For the rest of Black Elk's life he was a holy man and healer.

The vision journey continued with the horses from the four directions following him as the Grandfathers showed him how to use his powers to heal the sick including the animals, the people and the villages. When they came to the place where three rivers meet, "a place of mighty waters," they came to a blue man in flames. The four troops of horses could not overcome the blue man so they called on Eagle Wing Stretches, who was Black Elk, and he killed the blue man. Black Elk participated in the Battle of Little Bighorn a year later. The other warriors "count coup" on him (the prestigious act of touching the enemy with your weapon without being injured) and then the blue man turned into a harmless turtle. They came to a village with sick and dying people who they brought back to life and who joined him in planting the flowering stick in the center of the nation's sacred hoop. The stick turned into a cottonwood tree. They broke camp and headed north on the good red road.

The Four Ascents

As they headed north, he came to the four ascents, the four generations he would know. The first ascent was about Black Elk's life during the final decades of the Sioux tribe's life in the pre-conquest, non private property mode before the 1870s. The first ascent was green. They camped, formed the sacred circle as before and the cottonwood tree was OK.

The second ascent was steeper. People turned into animals. Black Elk turned into a soaring eagle over his people. The holy tree's leaves were falling. The second ascent evoked the time when wars engulfed his tribe until 1890 when defeat overtook them, when their lands were conquered, and the survivors confined to reservations. People turned into animals in their spiritual retreat to the world of the pre-conquest tribe. Black Elk fought in the wars as a 10 year old child, including the Battle of Little Bighorn where General Custer was defeated and killed.

The third ascent was the beginning of the difficulties.

> *"As they walked the third ascent, all the animals and fowls that were the people ran here and there, for each one seemed to have his own little vision that he followed and his own rules; and all over the universe I could hear wind at war like wild beasts fighting."* [6]

The third ascent evoked the times of disaster that befell not only his tribe but the entire world as World Wars I and II left their bloody marks. When they camped, the circle was broken and the sacred tree seemed to be dying. Rasaan Roland Kirk's lyrics "Everybody's moving in a different direction" came floating across my mind. I played it for my class, much to the bewilderment of everyone listening.

The fourth ascent saw the people who were animals turning back into people, thin and starving. The holy tree was gone. Black Elk wept as he saw this. The fourth ascent was marked by great fear. Black Elk was on his bay horse. He used his powers to heal, to raise up a skinny, sick black horse. The black horse became the chief of all the horses, beautiful and strong, and rallied the horses of the four quarters. They gathered in a circle and around the black horse who sang a song of great beauty, rallied the people and led all living creatures to the top of the fourth ascent. "Behold this day," says the grandfather, "for it is yours to make. Now you shall stand upon the center of the earth to see, for there they are taking you." Even amid the death and disasters of the twentieth century, Black Elk's vision found its way to the center of the Earth and the highest mountain. The riders of the West, North, East, and South appeared again and they all headed East once more, taking him to the highest mountain.

He returned to the six grandfathers who told him that by reaching the highest mountain he had triumphed. They gave him the gifts again, the cup of water, the bow and arrow, the powers to live and to destroy. They gave him the white wing of cleansing and the healing herbs, the sacred pipe and the flowering stick. They told him to return and use his powers well. Then, the nine year old Black Elk awakened in his parent's tepee. It is 1872. He told John Neihardt the story in 1934 and Joe Brown in 1947. He died in 1950.

By bringing his vision to Neihardt and Brown, his triumph began. It has taken me decades to understand the impact of this story on my rational western mind. I could have laughed it off as a "myth" of "primitive" people, ignoring its insights into the relationships we humans have with the earth. I could have ignored it and forgotten it as irrelevant to my life trying to find my way in mid twentieth century and now twenty-first century urban California. But it stays with me and comes back to me again and again as the decades pass and I witness the Earth continuing to age.

Black Elk's world view is in stark contrast to our western outlook. The dream, with the sacred woman in the center, placed humans in a co-equal status with all the animals and plants, not as masters of the universe with God given rights to do as they pleased. The dream made me aware of the spiritual reality that Black Elk and the Sioux people lived in. In contrast to the spiritual claims of monotheism which appeared hollow and oppressive to me, Black Elk's dream opened my awareness of my own spiritual connections to the earth around me, to horses, birds, rivers and rocks. I had experienced all these things and now I had a frame of reference to understand the inner feelings they evoked in me. These inner feelings became the basis for my attraction to pagan forms of understanding and released me from my "opium of the people" notion that, while true about monotheism, blinded me to the meaning and significance of my own inner spirituality.

Black Elk's dream was celebrated by his family and tribe in a ceremony which sanctified it and gave it the social recognition it deserved. The dream became the basis for his life of healing and wisdom that helped guide his people through the genocidal conquest and destructive wars that they experienced. In revealing the dream and its role in his life, he also revealed a philosophy of life and a way of being that stands on its own for the world to see. The story of the sacred woman at the center of it all provides us with an inkling of the possibilities outside the anti-woman monotheism that dominates most of the world today.

Still, I felt like I was stumbling blindly through his dream. The Goddess remained in the shadows of my awareness. My mind was still in the male only mode thinking about Neihardt and Brown, talking with Black Elk telling stories about his grandfathers. The sacred woman remained aloof, part of the village which suffered at the hands of men at war. It still felt like I was stuck in endless struggles between men over the earth.

Black Elk's dream offered me a new way of being as I faced the now confusing reality around me. I might have had a come to Jesus moment, or discovered God at a moment like this. But I did not. I might have fooled myself into believing I could adopt the Sioux religion and worship Wakan Tanka, the Great Spirit. But that did not appeal to me at all. I was in limbo and the only way out for me was to follow my inner reality, to stubbornly dig deeper into what was captivating me, no matter where it led.

I had taught this dream on my way out of the academic world. Students received it with their usual silence, like most things in classrooms structured for grades and diplomas. Was I just offering riddles and obscurity to cover my exit? My blindness had propelled me to uncover the light that Black Elk's dream shined on our reality. At that time, the students' blindness seemed overwhelming and impenetrable. To push deeper into the blindness, including my own, I ask myself was this the blindness that led Russell Means to conclude that we had proved ourselves unable to hear the voices of people like Black Elk and Russell Means? I was really participating in the blind leading the blind, and it was a dead end for me.

Sometime in the 1970's, before I quit academia, I had a prophetic dream of my own about how my brother, Steffen, and I were to part ways. We were both married with children at the time. One night I had a vivid, very strong and memorable dream. In the dream, we were driving up a narrow winding road into the Sierra mountains on our way to visit friends. Steffen and his wife were in the car with me and my family. It started to snow. We had to stop for gas at an old fashioned store front gas station with a wood overhang and two gas pumps straddled by wood posts holding up the roof. Steffen went inside as we pumped gas in the falling snow. He did not come out for a long time. Finally, I asked his wife, "What happened to Steffen?" She said, "He is not coming out." So I went into the gas station to see for myself. I found a big room with a long table full of nuns dressed in black and white habits sitting at the table. There were no priests or Brothers like at St. Mary's College where I had been working. Steffen was sitting at the head of the table next to a nun. "I'm staying," he told me. And that was the end of the dream.

Six months later, Steffen broke the news to me that he had joined the Catholic church. I was shocked. I shook my head in disbelief and blurted out, "I dreamt this!" I told him about my dream. He shrugged it off and we never spoke about it again until many years later. The dream wiped away any doubts I had about the reality of the spirit world and my own spirituality. The dream was not a message from God, I thought. It was a forecast of the future that foretold what was coming, just like Black Elk's dream had done. It was a message from the spirit world.

9: Leaving the Academic World

When I left academia, I slipped into the work-a-day world leaving all my confusion behind. Dust gathered on my books. While Black Elk's dream had helped me move away from academia, his dream was making waves across the country as students and teachers discovered it. Joe Brown moved on to teach at the University of Montana and Indiana University. He was one of the founders of the Native American Studies program that helped spread the interest in Native America across the country. I was not the only one fascinated by Black Elk's story. Yet, in the construction industry, where I was to spend the next three decades, no one even knew about it.

I was leaving a good friend behind and taking a different path. Having turned away from academia, including Black Elk's dream, I now faced more pressing matters deriving from making a living with my hands. His dream and the circle of the people froze in my mind and receded into the fuzzy world of memory.

As I learned to handle the elements of the earth in my new profession, I became more aware of my isolation from the radical movements of the past. But not just them. I fled society in general. My connections to other people continued to narrow in the silences that surrounded me. I no longer had a sounding board for my discontent which now took place quietly in my head.

The Rosenbergs

A memory from my academic years that haunted me still could not be silenced, however. I had studied economic history in University of Wisconsin, Madison graduate school in classes I shared with Michael Meeropol, the eldest son of Ethel and Julius Rosenberg. We became casually acquainted but never close enough for me to tell him about my feelings for the loss of his parents.

When I was 9 years old, his mother and father had been executed by the state of New York, accused of being Communist spies. I remember that moment well because I walked into the kitchen of our house in Oakland to find my mother crying while standing at the sink. She told me about the Rosenberg's execution then. It was a pivotal moment in the anti-communist crusade that burned itself into my memory as I watched my mother cry.

So years later on my way out of academia, back in the San Francisco Bay Area, I found myself determined to strike out at this anti-communist travesty by creating a media work that would support the now adult Rosenberg sons' efforts to vindicate their parents. I had developed an interest in creating media in my brief time in academia, making slide shows with music to illustrate course materials for students. In the pre-digital age it was all done with photos, slides, and tape recorders in live performances. Now I wanted to make a media work for a general audience outside academia about this terrible injustice that has burned itself into my soul so many years ago.

Meeting Nina Serrano

I needed help though. My rudimentary media skills were not up to making something that might get played on the TV or radio. So I called some of my old leftist contacts, asking if they knew anyone who could help me. And this is how I met my future wife and media collaborator, Nina Serrano. I learned about her work in Cuba on something called the Rosenberg Brigade that had toured a play about the Rosenbergs around the revolutionary island. I called her up and offered my help as an historian to create something like that for us here. She agreed and we met with her writing partner, Judith Binder, to create a play. We called it "The Story of Ethel and Julius Rosenberg." We wrote it all from the actual words of the Rosenbergs taken from their trial which I pulled out of the trial transcript itself. The play was performed on local stages and on public television at the time.

Nina introduced me to acting in this play as she assembled an experienced troupe of actors to put it on. She played the role of Ethel. I played the role of Ethel's brother, David Greenglass, who had betrayed her and sent her and Julius to the electric chair. Nina was the director of Community Theater Arts Workshop which put theater and television productions together for KQED's Open Studio and other outlets. I had no experience in theater or acting, but that was no problem for Nina, who mentored me through the basics, while working with our talented and experienced group of actors. We rehearsed together under Judith's direction which exposed me to the wonderful togetherness that actors and theater people share in the process of creating and performing plays. I had never experienced such total commitment and mutual support in a group before. It was a revelation to me after all my years in political groups with their back stabbing and factionalism during the murderous years of the war in Vietnam. It restored my soul much in the same way as acid had restored my spirit.

Becoming an actor introduced me to my own inner reality which actors call forth in creating a role. I could see what was in me but not be controlled by it. I didn't understand the deep impact this had on me until one day, after one of the performances of the play at La Peña in Berkeley. A childhood friend of mine had attended the play. Afterwards, she came up to me and told me she did not recognize me on stage as I played Ethel's traitorous brother. I was shocked. It showed me something about myself and the world around me I was unaware of. Spirit mattered and it changed things. It added another personal element to my appreciation of the spiritual world I began to glimpse in my studies of Black Elk.

Bringing forth my inner realities for a role in a play initiated a way of looking and seeing that was new to me. When our group of actors walked into a theater space, I saw the other performers sniff out the stage, the hall, the lights, the seats and so on. I had been oblivious to this kind of preparation. But now if I were to be a performer, I needed to know about the lights to control my appearance on the stage, the seats to know how to communicate with the audience and so on. I could see that I was connected to these spaces by intangible spirits that would be at play. I was stepping into a spiritual reality with Nina holding my hand.

But like the acid experience, the warm glow of the theater world soon faded as my academic salary stopped and my sporadic income from construction prodded me to devote myself to it more completely. However, I continued this spiritual practice of observation as a carpenter. It gave me an aesthetic, something I could feel, which helped me to design my work. In construction, this way of seeing is even more detailed because you have to go below the surface to see the structure of things. I was increasingly aware that the feeling evoked by any particular space derived from the labor that went into making it. This past labor lived in the spiritual reality of the place witnessed as people entered it. My brief theater training, along with my exposure to Black Elk's dream, carried me deeper and deeper into the spiritual dimensions of life. But it took decades for my brain to see it and my awareness to expand.

I also could see that the human experience within the built environment pushed the natural world away. We might walk on wooden floors but we didn't see the forests. What we do see of the forests is cut up and buried in the facade designed to serve humans. I saw that there was a dual reality at play. First, our domination of the natural world transformed it to serve human purposes. And second, the social and spiritual shaping of the human world occurred inside the room. As a professor in academia, I lived unquestioningly inside the room whose purpose, rather than its materials, shaped my existence. When I left academia and went into construction, I stepped into the world of doers who created these spaces. As the years went by, I could see that my impulses to build, especially when under an architect's direction, was in fact acting out the very thing that negated nature. I may have gained deeper knowledge of the materials and labor that went into creating the room. But my work contributed to our blindness to the natural world.

All construction projects of any size start with a bulldozer that obliterates the site scraping it down to bare earth. Then with the human intention supreme, the space is reconstructed to please the "client," the one with the money. I began to find the work more and more repugnant. I learned my trade over the years but eventually wandered away from it. My skills and sweat made someone rich but left me the same as I was when I started the job: broke and looking for work.

Big Mountain

During one of the lulls in my construction work, Nina was invited to join a small group of women in Oakland organizing to bring wool donated by weavers in Berkeley to the Navajo people on Big Mountain in Arizona. At the time I was driving a small pick up truck as most carpenters must. I offered to help them with my pick up, with me as the driver, to bring wool to the Navajo families there. The Hopi and Navajo were in dispute about who should occupy this area called Big Mountain. As part of this dispute, tribal authorities had confiscated the Navajo's sheep which were the source of their livelihood. We were bringing them fifteen hundred pounds of wool so they could continue to stay on Big Mountain, and to weave and sell products to survive.

I could see that Nina fit seamlessly into this group of spiritually enlightened women. I was very much on the outside of the group, feeling distrusted and isolated. Not unlike the feeling I might have if I walked into a hair salon full of women sitting under hair dryers. I shrugged it off and took my place as a helper and observer for Nina's benefit. It also helped that I was familiar with the Navajo area from my years at Verde Valley School. The women were keen not to permit any kind of male domination or male bias to enter their trip. At one stop along the road, I offered to pay for lunch but was not permitted to do so. What I thought was just a gesture of support was obviously more than that to them, and they would not permit it. It felt like a rejection, putting me in my place, whatever that might have been. It was unfamiliar territory because it hardly ever happened that way. I swallowed my pride but felt humiliated nevertheless.

After a two day drive from Oakland to Arizona, we arrived at Big Mountain. We were greeted cordially and unloaded the wool. Nina and I had planned to sleep in a tent for the night and then continue on our own to visit the beautiful places in the area like Monument Valley and Canyon de Chelly. As the night fell, the Navajo women invited the women of our group to a sweat bath. A special hut had been constructed for this. Nina agreed to join them and went off with them to the sweat lodge. I settled down in the tent expecting Nina to return shortly. However, it was dawn when she finally returned. She was clearly very much under the influence of the sweat and whatever ceremonies had taken place there. It was cold that night and she wore a puffy down jacket and every other piece of clothing she had. She walked stiffly and uncertainly back to the tent. We settled down for a while in the cab of the truck where I could see that she was in a special state, focused beyond us and almost unable to speak. She refused to get into the tent. Her other-worldliness scared me and I decided to get away from there immediately. We said our goodbyes and headed back down the mountain. It took Nina three days to come down from that experience and return to normal. We explored the beautiful Canyon de Chelly and drove by Monument valley. I drove her through Sedona to see Verde Valley School and then we headed back to the Bay Area.

It was an unforgettable experience even for me observing it from the outside. I don't know what the women experienced in that sweat lodge, but I do know that it was profound and uplifting. Months later, we received a small weaving made from the wool we had carried to Big Mountain. This weaving has hung on our wall ever since, reminding us of the journey. If I ever experienced the power of the Goddess, it was at Big Mountain. It became a deep anchor in my search for the missing elements in my view of history. Just as I had absorbed the reality of the spiritual world from the acid trip and from Black

Elk's dream, so now I absorbed the power of the Goddess. And just as I could not become an Indian or worshiper of Wakan Tanka, so now I remained outside the world of the Goddess. Nevertheless, I could not forget it. It became an inspirational source motivating me to continue to look more deeply into my historical understanding, propelling me to push ahead in my search for the Goddess and how her absence in our history contributed to our despiritualizing of the earth.

Up to this point, women had appeared in the historical narrative as bit players, marginally relevant to the direction of the story. All the stuff in Black Elk's dream about grandfathers and the sacred woman still left a hole in the narrative. The Goddess was in the shadows. Why have women been left out of our historical understanding? I believed that the arrival of private property was the cutting edge of cultural destruction faced by prehistoric people globally. Women faced the cruel results of conquest no less than the men who were enslaved and exiled from their lands. So before I went any further, I searched for direct testimony from women who had lived through this whole process of conquest. The voice of Sizani Ngubane, a South African woman who experienced such a conquest, made its impact on women crystal clear to me and provided a foundation for digging more deeply.

10: Private Property Arrives in South Africa: an Example

A South African woman, Sizani Ngubane, described how settler appropriation of the land impacted her and her people in South Africa. Ngubane described the transition to patriarchal private property that occurred in the late 19th century during her lifetime in South Africa in an essay in the book *Women and the Gift Economy, a Radically Different Worldview Is Possible*, edited by Genevieve Vaughan.

> *Pre-colonization, individuals could not own land. Land was regarded as a sacred gift from Umvelinqangi (The Creator). . . . Mother Earth was also regarded as a sacred home for our people who had passed on, and as the sacred source of food for the nation.*

> *In the past, communities stayed together and shared whatever resources they had. Mother Earth was regarded as a sacred gift and no one owned the land. People ploughed and tilled the land communally. The food that was produced from the land was shared among the families.*

> *When the youth who are looking after the livestock came back from the fields, they didn't have to go to their mother's kitchen to have their meals. They could go to any house in the community and find food ready for them. The heads of the households, usually men, were regarded as managers, but they could not make any decision without consulting their extended family, including the children (girls and boys). Even the children had a*

voice in how the cattle could be kept, and their voices were respected by the elders. Women had access to property and they were treated with respect.

Colonization left women without access to land. It took away communities' togetherness. People became individuals, and land became privately owned; Mother Earth was carved into small pieces. About 87 percent of this land went into the hands of the few white men, and the majority of the nation was left with only 13 percent of barren land on which to survive.

Before the land was taken away from the communities, the communities did not need to have money. People could survive without money. My mother told me that my grandfather sometimes worked for money for six month periods. Then he would come back and work at home, and it would be his brother's turn to earn money. They would negotiate among themselves who was to go and work for money that year, while the others continued to work at home on the land and take care of the livestock.[7]

The acquisition of her land was not gender neutral. Eighty seven percent of it ended up in the hands of a "few white men." The patriarchal racial nature of settler societies is front and center for her. Her description of the rise of individualism among her people that followed the expropriation of the land echoes Black Elk's description of the third ascent when his people scattered in all directions each with their own dream to pursue. Her description gave me a real picture of the process of conquest and its total destruction of the prehistoric social fabric that preceded it. What had been working for thousands of years was dissolved and dispersed in a matter of a few years. The impact of conquest was vast and devastating, tearing up the old world completely. The Goddess was pushed aside as women lost their central role in living on the land.

Being unaware of, and even hostile to, the cultures of indigenous people left conquerors blind to the impact of the conquest on all concerned, the conquerors and the conquered. It also left us blind about our own prehistoric roots. The more I looked at it, the more obvious it seemed to me that Europe's "rise" out of prehistory as "civilization" was the template for the later conquest of this continent that shaped how we treated prehistoric people here. What did we do? We obliterated them along with the natural world that supported them in a frenzy of conquest and destruction. We killed off millions of people. We destroyed millions of buffalo so the tribes could not eat. We dammed the rivers to submerge their lands. We gave them smallpox infected blankets to kill them off. And here in California, the government authorized their extermination by offering bounties for each dead Indian.

The conflict between Western values and the values of the indigenous cultures here in North America replayed what happened in our own prehistory. Central to it was the imposition of patriarchal private property on the people and lands being conquered. Blinded by the "Manifest Destiny" and religious dogma, we were repeating the same set of events here in the new world that had shaped us as a people in our own emergence as a civilization thousands of years earlier. Understanding this transformation has to start with what came before it, namely the cultures of prehistory.

Part 3: Woman Centered World of Prehistory

We must refocus our collective memory. The necessity for this has never been greater as we discover that the path of "progress" is extinguishing the very conditions for life on earth.

Marija Gimbutas, Preface to *Civilization of the Goddess.*

11. Marija Gimbutas: Refocusing Our Collective Memory

Even while working as a carpenter, I was wondering if there was a time when my ancestors were not settlers. Reviewing all of my college studies of history, I could not recall any evidence from modern, medieval, or ancient history that societies were anything but patriarchal, private property ruled, violent settler cultures. I was haunted by the fact that I could not escape my western European cultural heritage. I could not pay for lunch on our way to Big Mountain. And I could not join the tribal cultures that worshiped Wakan Tanka. Rejecting my own culture intellectually had made me unwilling to examine it more closely. Like, what's the point of studying all the history of the very world I found so repugnant? I had always focused on rebellion, on workers history, on the history of revolution. And yet, I continued singing the same old song, according to Russell Means. I had to look again and look deeper into it. And so I turned to prehistory to find out how it all started and what made us into a violent society, so full of hatred and war.

I started reading books about prehistory written by women which very quickly pointed me to the writings of Marija Gimbutas. She examined the nature of prehistoric societies. In her preface to *Civilization of the the Goddess*, Gimbutas examines

> *the way of life, religion, and social structure of the peoples who inhabited Europe from the 7th to the 3rd millennia B.C., which I have termed Old Europe, referring to Neolithic Europe before the Indo-Europeans. During this period, our ancestors developed settled agricultural communities, experienced a large growth in population, and developed a rich and sophisticated artistic expression and a complex symbolic system formulated around the worship of the Goddess in her various aspects.*[8]

I had always assumed that prehistory referred to a time before civilization. Gimbutas corrected this erroneous assumption. Prehistory refers to a time before writing which gives us a way to understand what happened in our past. Using information from interdisciplinary sources, Gimbutas found that:

> *Neolithic Europe was not a time "before civilization". . . It was, instead, a true civilization in the best meaning of the word. In the 5th and early 4th millennia B.C., just before its demise in*

east-central Europe, Old Europeans had towns with a considerable concentration of population, temples several stories high, a sacred script, spacious houses of four or five rooms, professional ceramicists, weavers, copper and gold metallurgists, and other artisans producing a range of sophisticated goods. A flourishing network of trade routes existed that circulated items such as obsidian, shells, marble, copper, and salt over hundreds of kilometers.

This civilization differed from our established views of civilization in two fundamental respects: 1. there was no war, and 2. it centered around the female Goddess.

It is a gross misunderstanding to imagine warfare as endemic to the human condition. Widespread fighting and fortification building have indeed been the way of life for most of our direct ancestors from the Bronze Age up until now. However, this was not the case in the Paleolithic and Neolithic. There are no depictions of arms (weapons used against other humans) in Paleolithic cave paintings, nor are there remains of weapons used by man against man.... The primordial deity for our Paleolithic and Neolithic ancestors was female, reflecting the sovereignty of motherhood. In fact, there are no images that have been found of a Father God throughout the prehistoric record. Paleolithic and Neolithic symbols and images cluster around a self-generating Goddess and her basic functions as Giver-of-Life, Wielder-of-Death, and as Regeneratrix. This symbolic system represents cyclical, nonlinear, mythical time.

The religion of the Goddess reflected a matristic, matrilineal, and endogamic social order for most of early human history. This was not necessarily "matriarchy," which wrongly implies "rule" by women as a mirror image of androcracy. A matrifocal tradition continued throughout the early agricultural societies of Europe, Anatolia, and the Near East, as well as Minoan Crete. The emphasis in these cultures was on technologies that nourished people's lives, in contrast to the androcratic focus on domination.[9]

So, from Gimbutas writings, I saw that female centered clans and cultures characterized humanity in western and world prehistory. Gimbutas' Goddess in prehistoric Europe had the same essential features as described in Black Elk's dream. Black Elk's sacred woman was part of this global culture. The grandfathers' gifts to Black Elk were the power to live (water), the power to destroy (bow and arrow) and the power to heal. As Gimbutas wrote: "self-generating Goddess and her basic functions as Giver-of-Life, Wielder-of-Death, and as Regeneratrix." In spite of the swirling controversy and endless denials I encountered in archaeological and historical literature, I could only conclude that all patriarchal civilizations arose out of this female centered prehistoric world.

It made all the difference for me to comprehend the primacy of the female roots of all patriarchal civilizations. If you assumed patriarchy and private property always existed, then you could argue that the rise of civilization was a linear development, rising like a plant grows from the ground, which is basically how the mainstream looks at it. But if you understand the rise of patriarchal civilization as the negation of prehistory and the suppression of the female Goddess, it transforms your understanding of patriarchal civilization. I could see that war and conquest were the engines of transformation. Patriarchy was synonymous with the arrival of war and the suppression of women.

How, I wondered, could the primacy of the Goddess in prehistory stay hidden from me until now? The rise of feminist reinterpretations of our past had revealed it, potentially removing the blinders for all those ready to see. I had gone through two universities history departments, earned my PhD and yet never had occasion to confront this hidden fact. I had stuck to my rebellious roots for decades, joined the working class, worked with my hands and still remained blind. Now, seeing the female roots of civilization, I came to the realization that our society's blindness to nature and hostility to women are the same thing, tied together inextricably. My inability to transcend these roots places me undeniably inside Russell Means' chorus singing the same old song. I had to look more deeply into our female roots. How did the universal female goddess come to dominate prehistory?

12: Woman as an Evolutionary Force

Without understanding the role of women in our evolution, I could see how Darwin's theories were reduced to the "survival of the fittest" idea with men wielding clubs and spears, killing all the animals and each other and dragging women around by their hair. Male bias in our settler society has shaped our views of evolution to explain how human society evolved. "Man" is then seen as the highest creation of the evolutionary process, once more leaving women out of the process, and providing justifications for our destructive patriarchal behaviors.

Monica Sjöö and Barbara Mor, from their book *The Great Cosmic Mother*, helped me see how these male assumptions blinded me to the abundant evidence of women's role in our evolution.

> *Woman is not comprehended as an evolutionary or evolutionizing creature. . . . This, despite the known fact that among contemporary and historic hunting-and-gathering people, as among our remote hunting-and-gathering ancestors, 75 percent to 80 percent of the group's subsistence comes from the women's food-gathering activities. This, despite the known fact that the oldest tools used by contemporary hunters and gatherers, and the oldest, most primal tools ever found in ancient sites, are women's digging sticks. This, despite worldwide legends that cite women as the first users and domesticators of fire. This, despite the known fact that women were the first potters, the first weavers, the first textile-dyers and hide-*

> *tanners, the first to gather and study medicinal plants— i.e., the first doctors— and on and on.*

I could see plainly that women's work was fundamental to the creation and survival of early human societies. But Sjöö and Mor place women deeper in the evolutionary process when they reveal her role in the creation of language, science and religion.

> *Observing the linguistic interplay between mothers and infants, mothers and children, and among work-groups of women, it is easy to speculate on the female contribution to the origin and elaboration of language. That the first time measurements ever made, the first formal calendars, were women's lunar-markings on painted pebbles and carved sticks is also known. And it is thoroughly known that the only "God-image" ever painted on rock, carved in stone, or sculpted in clay, from the Upper Paleolithic to the Middle Neolithic—and that's roughly 30,000 years— was the image of a human female.* [10]

Putting women into the process of the evolution of our species shined a bright light on the male biases of my world. How could she have been left out? How could we deny that human awareness arose out of the evolutionary role of women? And how could we miss that her role in prehistory made the female Goddess supreme for 30,000 years? How could all the "great minds" of history have missed this? And what motivates us to continue to deny it?

Monica Sjöö and Barbara Mor wrote their incisive critiques of the patriarchal domination of our thinking while they were homeless and destitute in the 1970s. They were not playing some academic game adding more lines to their resumes in writing their book. No, excluded, rejected and vilified, these two women rose up from destitution in an act of rebellion and self affirmation to describe the central role of women in pre patriarchal societies. The dire situation out of which their writing emerged gave them more credibility to me than any diploma on the wall or suffixes after their names.

Their appreciation of the role of women in prehistory gave me a better understanding of the human family and sexual relations in the formative era of our existence.

Among most preliterate people— as among the ancient Paleolithic and Neolithic peoples— the man's role in procreation is seen as one of "opening" the womb; but it is believed that children are placed in the mother's womb by spirits— perhaps the returning spirits of dead kin. The man cannot relate to the children as his property, in other words; they come from the mother, through the mother, and belong to the spirit world. There are fewer emotional conflicts in such cultures; the neurosis-producing, ego-festering hothouse atmosphere of the Victorian-type nuclear family is entirely avoided. After spending early childhood close to the mother's body, the young child then moves out into the group's life, guided by the social father. The child belongs to the whole people, and feels this belonging.

I especially appreciated their description of the role of the father, freed from the power-mad prison of patriarchy, as a nurturing force living in harmony with a society that had no orphans.

Because he does not relate egoistically or possessively to the children, the social father is much better prepared to let his own nurturing talents develop truly; there is no question of property right, personal ambition, economic responsibility, sexual jealousy, or social status involved in his relationship to women and children. These cultures are not perfect, but the notorious soap opera of Western domestic life is avoided. Most of all, these matrifocal cultures weave a webwork of non-possessive intergroup relationships, which supports a growing being through every phase and crisis of unfolding life.[11]

13: The Evolution of Our Physiology

I soon realized that women's role in our evolution went deeper, beyond social life and culture, into our physiology as a species. I became aware of the unique characteristics of human birth compared to other primates. Human babies are born facing the mother's back. All other primates give birth with the new born facing front or side. This unique feature allowed passage of a large brain from the womb into the world in our species which walks upright on two feet. When giving birth, other primate females can reach down and grasp the newborn to help in the birth process.

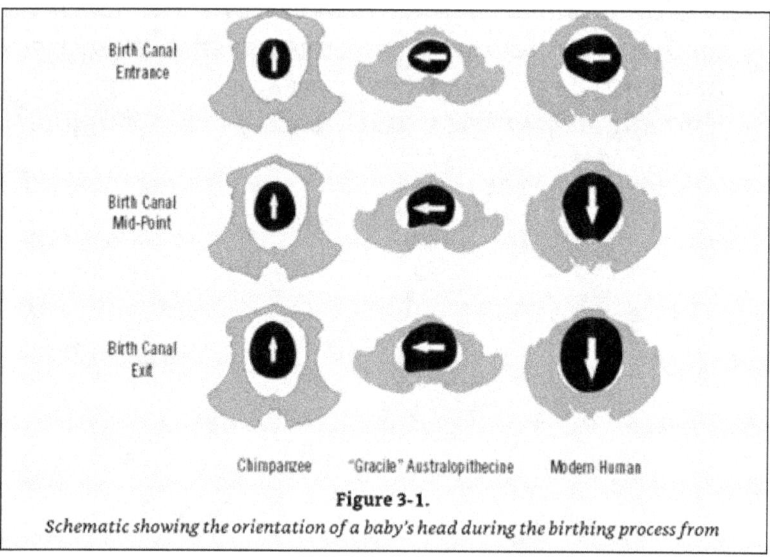

Figure 3-1.

Schematic showing the orientation of a baby's head during the birthing process from

For more on human parturition, see
https://newlifeinburiedbones.wordpress.com/2014/12/19/
anatomy-and-behavioral-strategies-of-human-and-
nonhuman-primate-parturition/

With the fetus facing to the back, the mother can injure the fetus if she pulls it towards her in the birth process. This evolutionary change in the anatomy of the human female certainly contributed to the socialization of birthing and the role of the midwife.

It seemed obvious to me, then, that evolving over thousands of years, female anatomy was a driving force bringing social life into the genetic makeup of our species. As socialized birthing contributed to the survival of our species, language and communication skills grew as the brain and muscles of the face and mouth evolved to facilitate talking and other interactions necessary for successful births. Socialized birthing spread to human cultures globally as our species numbers grew. The evolution of the female body explained to me how the social process of human culture weaved its way into the evolution of our genetic makeup.

The physiology of birth was only the start. The central role of women in the rise of human culture unfolded in front of me as I followed Monica Sjöö and Barbara Mor's description of the role of women in prehistoric life after birth:

> *In the beginning, the first environment for all new life was female: the physical/ emotional/ spiritual body of the mother, and the communal body of women—young girls, grown women, older women—working together. When hunting-and-gathering people move, the infant is carried bound close to the mother's body; when they settle, the women form an "inner circle" campsite of women and children. The socialization process begins here.*

The early years of life shape human infants fundamentally in our relationship to our mothers. Women understand this. But men, including myself, have trouble grasping the implications of this key aspect of our emergence as individuals. Our vision and memory are fogged over by the wall of patriarchal bias we must all pass through to reach adulthood. I could imagine that this was not the case in our prehistory, before patriarchy arrived. And this awareness and appreciation of the female creative center of society, it seemed to me, must lay behind the creation of hundreds of thousands of clay prehistoric Goddess figures globally.

> *Human culture is marked by a strengthening and prolongation of the relation between mothers and offspring. For its first year the human child is virtually an "embryo" outside the womb, extremely vulnerable and totally dependent. Female group behavior—the cooperative care-sharing among mothers and children, older and younger women, in the tasks of daily life—emerges from the fact of this prolonged dependence of the human child on the human female for its survival.*

This core experience of life within the circle of mothers and women dictated the roles of men and the social imperatives within all human cultures.

> *Males help— but they also leave; the male body comes and goes, but the female presence is constant. Females train, discipline, and protect the young; beyond infant care, the maintenance and leadership of the entire kin-group is the task of women. The female animal is always on the alert, for on her rests*

the responsibility not only of feeding the young, but of keeping the young from being food for others. She is the giver and also the sustainer of beginning life. Among humans, males help with protection and food acquisition; but it is the communal group of females that surrounds the child, in its first four to six years of life, with a strong physical, emotional, traditional, and linguistic presence. And this is the foundation of social life and human culture.

The inner circle of women made possible the successful propagation of our species over tens of thousands of years of prehistory. Patriarchal bias blinded us to all this, creating untenable alternative ideas about the origins of human culture. Sjöö and Mor put it this way:

The popular image of early human society as being dominated—indeed created—by sexist male hunters and ferocious territorial head-bangers just doesn't hold water. If the first humans had depended solely on despotic and aggressive male leaders, or on several males in chronic, ritualistic contention for power— human society would never have developed. Human culture could never have been invented. The human presence on earth would never have evolved.

Patriarchy stripped away the role of women from our understanding of evolution, making the suppression and denial of the Goddess necessary. But such denial is hard to maintain since it flies in the face of the universal experience of us all being born from our mothers.

> *The fact is that it was from this first inner circle of women— the campsite, the fire-site, the cave, the first hearth, the first circle of birth—that human society evolved. As hominids evolved into Paleolithic Homo sapiens, and then into settled and complex Neolithic village people on the time-edge of "civilization," these tens of thousands of years of human culture were shaped and sustained by communities of creative, sexually and psychically active women— women who were inventors, producers, scientists, physicians, lawgivers, visionary shamans, artists. Women who were also the Mothers—receivers and transmitters of terrestrial and cosmic energy.[12]*

So after reading all this, I understood the central place of women in the cultures of prehistory. For many millennia, Goddess centered human cultures grew out of the physical capabilities of homo sapiens, with our brains, our hands and our reproductive behaviors. We arose out of our evolutionary past as social behavior became genetically lodged in our bodies, centered on women and the birthing process. Social life and language within the protected hearth where babies were born is how our species perpetuated itself.

I had to ground my view of prehistoric culture in my understanding of the physical evolution of our species which required a social group. Social life and language arose along with this necessity and women did it. Language and social cohesion became the tools of homo sapiens reproduction, as necessary as the opposable thumb, the erect posture and large brain, for species survival.

14: The Advent of Private Property

Now, I could see how human nature grew out of the vast millennia of time centered on female goddess worshiping cultures of prehistory. It was an era of peace built around the central role of the female forces of creation. Inside the Goddess cultures, reaching every corner of the world with millions of inhabitants, human societies learned how to domesticate plants and animals inside the village life that arose with it. With productivity and population growing, there was a time in the early Neolithic period, before private property, that human civilizations existed without war. The earth was sacred and our relations with all forms of life acknowledged and upheld by the wisdom of our elders. This might seem utopian and idealistic in the context of our world today. But the evidence supports it. And it is fundamental to understanding what ended it.

Trade had always been part of prehistoric cultures. But when humans transitioned from nomadic hunters and gatherers to settled village life supported by agriculture, a new possibility arose. The surpluses from growing domesticated plants and animals around settled villages, combined with trade, opened the door to wealth and plenty that the world had never seen before. It was like letting a genie out of the bottle that would never go back in.

In this context, men began to take possession of the land within the framework of the female oriented world. Taking individual possession of the land allowed men to keep the wealth created from it instead of allowing the wealth to flow back to the women centered clans and collective villages that had traditionally claimed it.

Private property first arose out of the physical act of conquering the land, fencing it in, denying the mother right, and using it to create wealth for an individual male owner and their male heirs. It was the foundation of patriarchy from the outset. Once land was confiscated in this manner, the doors to competition and theft were open for all men to grab some for themselves. Taking physical possession of the land created islands of exclusion which gradually displaced the surrounding cultures. This act of "privatization" lays at the heart of ancient and modern social classes and all the evils associated with them: inequality, misogyny, slavery, racism, exploitation, violence, oppression and war.

Timetable of Private Property

This conceptual portrayal of the rise of private property came to me as I began to integrate our female origins into my view of the broad sweep of human existence on our planet. How did this transition from the Goddess centered prehistory to patriarchal civilization, I wondered, occur as an actual, historical sequence of events?

I put some known dates into this broad framework to envision what such a timetable might look like. I understood that ancient Greek (patriarchal) myths were in place 2500 years before the Bible, which appeared around 500 BC. The ancient myths of Greece appeared around 3000 BC. Civilizations first arose some 5000 years before the Greek myths, or around 8000 BC. By this reckoning, the transition to private property took place over three to four thousand years leading up to the first patriarchal civilizations, or in rough terms, eight to twelve thousand years ago.

Rise of Private Property: 12 – 8,000 BC

First Patriarchal Civilizations: 8000 BC

Greek Myths: 3000 BC

Bible: 500 BC

The Goddess reigned 12,000 years ago and for countless millenniums before that. Private usurpation of the land began after that time. Greek myths, appearing five thousand years ago, gave expression to the world view of patriarchal civilizations. During this transitional period, both types of human culture existed side by side, with private property expanding at the expense of the non-owning Goddess centered lands and cultures. The continuation of this "privatization" process today puts a new light on indigenous cultures and their potential to help us find our way out of the dead end we are in. If patriarchy is the disease killing us, then civilization is the metastasized version driving us to the end. Indigenous cultures may contain the cure.

I asked myself why didn't Russell Means' challenge embrace the Goddess origins of humanity? It may be a reflection of the fact that the 1980 meeting in which he issued his challenge was a meeting within the patriarchal world. His challenge was directed at European men, man to man. The female oriented prehistoric world was not part of the picture. He made no distinction between our patriarchal present and our female centered prehistory, when the European world existed in harmony with nature for thousands of years. Means was observing our blindness to nature as he knew it at that time. However, now it is clear to me that our blindness to the need to respect nature turns out to be the same thing as our blindness to the role of women in our evolution, our prehistory, and the origins of our species. The suppression of women is inextricably linked to our inability to respect the natural world. Russell Means' challenge led me to this conclusion.

Part 4: Where Marx and Engels Went Wrong

Marxism is a patriarchal philosophy. That is my conclusion after reviewing how I traveled through the decades without discovering the Goddess and without realizing that I was singing Russell Means' same old song. I had to look more closely at Marxism to understand how this happened and what it means. It follows from dispiritualizing the Earth, something Marxists and non-Marxists alike have fallen into.

Human spirituality in prehistory, before private property, was not a separate subject from the rest of life. It was part of everything and it was in everything. People who shared this holistic spirituality faced disaster when they became slaves and workers inside civilization. The earth no longer appeared as the sacred source of life that had nourished their indigenous ways and cultures when they lived freely on the land. Now, the land became the fenced in farm or factory in which they had to give up their time and effort in order to eat. The powers who ruled this new way of life came along with black robed priests who offered a different kind of religion to help the new captives conform and survive. Human relationships to the earth had changed and with that change came a new mindset that dispiritualized the earth itself.

Marx and Engels viewed religion as "the opium of the people," correctly identifying the role of monotheism in subduing the rebellious spirits of the oppressed. This new role of religion arose inside civilizations as human beings adapted to the new power of the property owning classes and their monotheistic god. But it is a mistake to subsume human spirituality under the umbrella of male gods. My own spiritual journey outside all religious institutions demonstrated this to me. Becoming aware of the Goddess, the forces of creation all around me, had nothing to do with anyone's god in the sky. I could recognize the Goddess from my own experiences and I had to assume that humanity has also been doing this since prehistory.

Human spirituality focusing on the Goddess was universal in the eons before patriarchal monotheism, and throughout the millenniums of the early neolithic period. This neolithic transitional period is when the war against the Goddess started and the despiritualization of the earth began. It is also the period when private property spread globally and women fell under the oppressive new patriarchal family structure of monogamy. When humanity stepped across this threshold into the culture of private property, we began our journey into the ecological crisis that we now confront. Monotheism and monogamy cannot be separated from it. We left behind the old spiritual space with its global unity and entered into a new spiritual space that blinded us to our past.

15: Despiritualizing the Earth

I spent many decades believing that the problems of our society stemmed from capitalism. Now here was Russell Means saying that was not really true. Instead he pegged it on despiritualizing the earth, an orientation that impacted Marxists and non Marxists alike. Russell Means saw it as a form of insanity:

> In terms of the despiritualization of the universe, the mental process works so that it becomes virtuous to destroy the planet. Terms like progress and development are used as cover words here, the way victory and freedom are used to justify butchery in the dehumanization process. For example, a real-estate speculator may refer to "developing" a parcel of ground by opening a gravel quarry; development here means total, permanent destruction, with the earth itself removed. But European logic has gained a few tons of gravel with which more land can be "developed" through the construction of road beds. Ultimately, the whole universe is open — in the European view — to this sort of insanity.

> I do not believe that capitalism itself is really responsible for the situation in which American Indians have been declared a national sacrifice. No, it is the European tradition; European culture itself is responsible. Marxism is just the latest continuation of this tradition, not a solution to it. To ally with Marxism is to ally with the very same forces that declare us an acceptable cost.[13]

The spirit world and the world of Marxist rebellion had floated separately in my inner world for many years. Imagining radical workers storming the citadels of capitalism never included the indigenous people outside town. And besides Joan of Arc, it also never included women, although I knew there were women in all of our rebellions. It seemed as if I had been living within the world that Means was attacking all the years of my life. And now I could see that I was living in the world of patriarchy that was based on negating the spirit world, the spirit world of the Goddess.

Growing Doubts

Marxism came along with my experiences growing up as a red diaper baby in Oakland in the 1940's and 1950's. (see Chapter 3: 'Marxism in My blood') My loyalty to it remained strong even after I could no longer fit many of my life experiences into my old views of the world.

Doubts about Marxism grew during the decades of the 1980's and 90's. The collapse of the Soviet Union in 1991 created some doubts, but the impact of the collapse on my father created even more. Much of my faith in Marxism derived from the hope embodied in the existence of the socialist USSR, hopes I shared with my father. But these hopes seemed to be fading in my life which was filled with physical work, sometimes as a wage worker and others as a small business owner on the verge of failure.

Isolated from the remnants of the radical movements I had embraced for so many years, I nevertheless clung to my loyalty to Marxism and to the causes of the lower depths of society still struggling against poverty and oppression. My desire for revolutionary change did not go away. I cheered our victories and booed our defeats. I could no more climb the economic ladder of success on the backs of the oppressed than I could start worshiping Wakan Tanka or join the born again religious fanatics whooping it up in their Christian churches. Inside me, rebellion continued to coexist with spirituality like two separate worlds that would not connect up. And the longer it went on, the more it created a crisis within me. With my academic years faded into the past, and my cultural alienation engulfed in clouds of marijuana smoke, I was ripe for a family intervention, of sorts.

Family Intervention

It happened one day in the summer of 1985 when my father invited me to take possession of his films and photo collection which he had accumulated over two decades in his work as a documentary photographer, 1958-1978.[14] He was motivated to get rid of his collection because people kept calling him asking to use his images in their films, books, magazines, and museums. He wanted nothing to do with the licensing and archiving of his work. With my background in history, I was primed to take up the task. The rise of the digital world in these decades would have meant little to me driving around in my pick up doing home repairs if it had not been for the boxes of my father's films.

His films were dear to my heart. Not only did he film civil rights and anti-war protests I had marched in during my undergraduate years at UC Berkeley. He also filmed the police dragging me out of the lobby of the luxurious San Francisco Sheraton Palace hotel in 1964 during our sit-in against their racist hiring policies.[15] He made films for farm workers' unions, for the movement against the war in Vietnam, and for environmental groups on forestry, mining and the San Francisco Bay. And I couldn't forget our films on the USSR which lay there in my memory forever linking me to my socialist roots.

My father had searched out the front lines of the 1960's protest movements in the times before the arrival of the smart phone that made everyone a documentary photographer. Using "analog" technology—cameras, film stock and old fashion film and sound editing—he provided films and photos to support protest movements that needed some good publicity because they were being systematically ignored and vilified by the mainstream media.[16] After he retired, his collection became a valuable archive of 1960's protest movements. His images have stayed in demand over all the years since he decided to give it to me.

He said, "Either you take them, or I will throw them overboard in a gunny sack," reverting to the language of his merchant seaman days of the 1930's when he had steered merchant ships through the Golden Gate before the bridge was built. The immediate motivation for getting rid of it all was the mounting number of insistent and sometimes annoying phone calls from film makers and editors wanting to use his footage in their productions. Not to mention the haggling over how much to charge, how to handle the material, how to secure them from being stolen and so on. He wanted nothing to do with it. I agreed to take it all.

It wasn't a simple handover, however. First, we went to a lawyer and drew up papers establishing my ownership of the copyright and the materials themselves. I set up a business for handling the continuing inquiries which I called Estuary Press.[17] I made business cards and opened a business checking account. I vowed from the outset that the archive would be a business or it would go into that gunny sack and overboard. I was not going to give it away like my father had done for so many years.

Accepting his collection launched me into a new phase in my life. I felt like he was handing me an anchor to my past, to the radicalism that had long since floated downstream in my life. I said to myself, ok, mainstream, you go ahead and train the youth to conform to our rotten society. I will use my training and historical skills to preserve the very thing you want to forget. The hand-over of his collection occurred at about the same time as TV stations decided to throw out all their archives over 10 years old which pretty much summed up our society's attitude towards our past, radical or not.

My father had dedicated himself, with the support of his wife Alice, to making these films and photos for the good of the movements of protest and rebellion, until their money and energy ran out. He used to buy release prints of his films to give to organizers where they often ended up roasting in the trunk of a movement car somewhere along the road after the activists were arrested and carted off to jail. He insisted that the organizers pay the cost of the print when he could. When I received the collection, it was known mainly to other photographers who knew Harvey and had witnessed his photographic activism over the years.

I had no money to continue my dad's largess. Either the collection paid for itself or it would disappear. I felt slightly guilty insisting that it had to be a business. Alice and Harvey accepted the idea without a protest but with a little pity thrown in, pity for the naïve idea that it could make money. The work of cataloging and archiving the collection focused my attention not only on the radical protests themselves. It also focused me on the faces, bodies, and outfits of those times. It became an important step in my journey to understand the spirit of that time and the way the spirit moves through us in the modern world.

My training as an historian sprang back to life. It was the tail end of the era of film as I sat down with my dad's reel to reel viewer and examined it all. I cataloged twenty two film and file drawers full of eight and a half by eleven inch manila envelopes full of negatives.[18] I labeled the boxes and envelopes so I could actually find things if people called. Harvey had processed his film at Monaco Labs in San Francisco which maintained a climate controlled vault for filmmakers. For the first years of my possession of the films, they sat safely in Monaco's vault. Monaco's went out of business due to the rapid rise of digital technology that reduced film photography to a shadow of its former self, much like automobiles did for horses. When Monaco's closed its doors, I took everything home and constructed a special room in the house to keep it all.

Besides the reels and canisters full of film elements, I cataloged the still photo collection Harvey had created in his garage dark room.[19] He filmed farm worker protests, anti war protests, civil rights protests, including sharecroppers in Mississippi in 1963 and 1964 risking their lives to register to vote.[20] He took still photos during his filming trips whenever he could. I decided to make a book from these photos which I called *Critical Focus*.

The title was the suggestion of Katie Peake, Alice's sister and Harvey's sister in law, who was also an avid supporter of the farm worker's unions. We were all standing around in the kitchen one afternoon wondering what to call the book when Katie made the suggestion. It rang true and I immediately adopted it as the title of the book. Published in 1987, *Critical Focus: The Black and White Photographs of Harvey Wilson Richards*, made Estuary Press into something more than a business arrangement for licensing photography.[21] I had stumbled into a "sideline" that would eventually change me from a carpenter to a publisher and consume my attention for the rest of my life. It also propelled me into the digital revolution that quickly put Harvey's films on a global platform. From the outset, my publishing was about more than words. It was about images and films.

But don't get me wrong. Words were fundamental to the whole endeavor. Once I realized what I could do with the photo collection on my computer and on the web, I decided to find out if I could also publish books with the same tools.

My wife, Nina Serrano, presented me with the perfect opportunity to find out. She had been writing poetry since 1969 and had hundreds of poems all stuffed into her filing cabinet. I asked her if she had any poems she wanted to make into a book. She disappeared into the other room and soon returned with a stack of poems she plunked down on my desk. After much wrangling, these stacks of paper turned into the *Heart Suite Trilogy*, three books that collected her poetry written over the years from 1969 to 2012. She had published a book of poems in 1969 with Pocho Che Publishers in San Francisco called *Heart Songs, Collected Poems 1969 -1979*. I created an ebook to make it available today. Then, *Heart's Journey, Selected Poems 1980-1999* and *Heart Strong, Selected Poems, 2000-2012* came out. We also unearthed her notebooks full of drawings from these same years. The drawings fit perfectly along with the poetry and so we included them as color images in the *Heart Suite Trilogy*.[22]

The next step was to figure out how to offer these books as publish-on-demand paperbacks (no more boxes of books for us) and ebooks on Amazon, Google, Barnes and Noble, Kobo and elsewhere.[23]

As a result of all this digital publishing work, I established a website for Nina (https://estuarypress.com/nina-serrano-homepage/) where her poetry books, her theater work, films and other writings found a home.[24] My admiration and love of her writings and her creative genius contributed greatly to my growing awareness of the Goddess living all around me.

At the dawn of the digital age, I began to scan my father's photos into my computer. I started digitizing them in the 1990's, but the effort really took off in the early 2000's. My first computers were purchased for my construction businesses in the 1980's, but the potential of computers for Estuary Press was obvious from the start. I converted all the films to video cassettes, then to digital files. I established an Estuary Press website (https://estuarypress.com)[25] and along with it the Harvey Richards Media Archive website (https://estuarypress.com/harvey-richards-media-archive-home/).[26] The first version of the website was very rudimentary. Just a placeholder web page with a photograph and a phone number on it. It was like having a plastic bag full of water with a guppy in it. If I wanted the fish to live, I had to get an aquarium, sand, plants, filters, food, and so on.

As I scanned the films and photos into the computer, I was also learning how to handle video and still images for the web. File sizes grew rapidly along with the speed and capacity of computers. Once I had all 22 of Harvey's films in the computer, I figured out how to edit short preview clips from each film. In 2005, YouTube arrived and I created a channel (https://www.youtube.com/channel/UCjLntHEno-2ygOiD0fOl0Aw) which allowed me to post these short previews online and then embed them on my growing website where the films could be purchased.[27] All of a sudden, Estuary Press and Harvey's photography could be accessed from anywhere on the planet. I was amazed at what I had stumbled into and wished my father had lived to see it.

Estuary Press' website became an access point that brought producers of films, videos, books, and exhibits from all over the world to the photo collection. The film projects that have used his footage and images include many well known films, from groundbreaking documentaries like "Berkeley in the Sixties" and "Eyes on the Prize", to feature films like "Fear and Loathing in Las Vegas."[28] His photographs are exhibited at museums all over the country including the Smithsonian, as well as in National Monuments like the Cesar Chavez National Monument in Keene, California. The income from licensing has financed the costs of all this work.

Socialism and Marxism were never very far from the surface of all this. In a nutshell, my father's and my Marxist affinity for protest and opposition to war and injustice was, of course, the underlying motivation for preserving the collection and putting it on the web. Working on it in the 2000s in the context of the disastrous decline in our educational system and the deep distortions of history resulting from book banning and political censorship, I had come to believe that the real history of protest and dissent would never be believed unless people could see it. Putting the photos and films on the web was one way to do it.

While creating the preview clips, I came to Harvey and Alice's 1961 films on the USSR. These two films chronicled our visit to the Soviet Union when I was 17, focusing on the conditions of women and children in a socialist society.[29] I wondered if I should really bother with these films on the USSR at all. It was in the 1990's just as the USSR collapsed and the insufferable arrogance of the anti-communists was everywhere. I said to myself, what the hell, I can't leave them out. So I made a clip which I called "Ordinary Life in the USSR" and put it up on YouTube, along with all the previews of the other films.

Much to my surprise, "Ordinary Life in the USSR" took off like a rocket. It is now 2022 and these clips have received over a million views. The "Ordinary Life" video preview alone has received over 800,000 views in 120 countries around the globe and continues to attract thousands of new views every month. I realized that in spite of the collapse of the USSR, socialism and the condition of women and children continued to be an important topic on the minds of many around the world.

Among the viewers of "Ordinary Life in the USSR" was University Professor Kristen Ghodsee who contacted me to acquire the two films on women and children in the USSR for her classes. Ghodsee is the author of many books on women in Eastern Europe during the transition from socialism back to capitalism. I first became aware of Ghodsee when I read her book *The Left Side of History*. I liked it so much I reviewed it on my website in a review entitled "The Left Side of History: The Left Side is My Side."[30]

From this book, focusing on Bulgaria, I learned that the Soviet backed socialist government of Bulgaria made significant improvements in the conditions of women and children with the adoption of a Family Code (1985) that implemented nation-wide programs of child care, family leave and women's restroom facilities in all workplaces. It put what I had seen in the Soviet Union during our 1961 trip into a broader perspective of how socialist societies impacted women and children generally. When eastern European communism was overthrown in 1989, free enterprise assumed command and these advances slipped into the past. Ghodsee, I wrote, "likens communism to Cassandra, the mythical prophet in the *Iliad* who foretold the future but was not believed and, therefore, ignored. It is a great analogy for understanding the legacy of the socialist experiments that briefly ruled eastern Europe."

What communism was prophesying, I can see now, was that the condition of women and children depended on the control of private property. As socialist governments brought private property under social and political control, the voices of women rose and society began to redress grievances that had accumulated in the long standing suppression of women in western societies and beyond. It did not happen so much because the Communist Parties made it a part of their programs, which they did. It happened because the voices of women combined with the advocates of justice to make it happen. Ghodsee made me realize that the advances experienced by women and children during the socialist era happened because of the activism and advocacy of the women themselves. This resonated with my understanding of how slavery had been abolished in the US during the civil war. The role of the slaves themselves was central to abolition, a fact much denied and suppressed in the mainstream version of our history.[31]

Even though the socialist governments were still firmly in the hands of the patriarchal world order, socialist measures weakened private property enough to allow women to break through. When the socialist governments of eastern Europe collapsed in the 1990's, the barriers went back up and women and children fell back into the shadow of patriarchy. And certainly this lesson has been ignored by the world just like Cassandra's prediction with grave consequences for women and society as a whole.

In documenting this process and interviewing many women who had lived through socialism, Ghodsee gave me a new perspective with which to view Marxism, its promise and impact during the brief triumph of socialism in eastern Europe. It also made me aware that Marxism had never escaped the grip of patriarchy which reasserted itself vigorously after the fall. I did not attribute this vigorous reassertion of patriarchy to some western conspiracy or from the insidious influence of the CIA. No, it was a patriarchal culture that I was seeing. It seemed to me that it was the same thing that Russell Means was seeing when he observed that Europeans had proved themselves unable to respect nature. This may seem to be an overly ambitious conclusion, but to me it made total sense. The immovable cultural practice of despiritualizing the Earth appears to me in exactly the same way as patriarchal contempt for women. Both are like the elephant in the room. In the long view, they operate under the radar of our consciousness, controlling us and the direction of our history in exactly the same way.

16: Marxism in Perspective

My father's suicide in April, 2001, when he was 89 and I was 67, removed the last barriers against thinking about where Marx and Engels went wrong. I was not going to be an anti-Marxist because none of our problems came from Marxism. The adversarial nature of the US's anti-communist milieu had left me with the scars of stubborn resistance that I could not shake, until then. My father came to the end of the road after 9 years being partially paralyzed with a stroke and finally with a knee injury on his good knee that left him bedridden. Like a boxer softened up with a body attack, all that was left to finish him off was the right hook to the chin. That blow was the collapse of the Soviet Union and the seeming triumph of the capitalist/imperialist system he had fought against his whole life. It was a terrible blow for him. And it left me wondering how to understand it. I knew that something basic in my father's world had been crushed and that struck me as hard as anything else. The Marxism he had relied upon had let him down. My unquestioned allegiance to Marxism died with him. I could not ignore this failure.

In retrospect, I can see that what failed for my father was not so much Marxism. What failed was the historical project that the Soviet Union represented to him and his whole generation of radicals. The Soviet Union was born out of the Russian Revolution of 1917, five years after Harvey was born. It lasted his whole life (almost), providing leadership during the war against fascism and during his union organizing during the 1930s and 1940s. He shot himself with the 38 caliber pistol that years ago he had carried in his back pocket as the chief union steward in the 1946 strike in the San Francisco shipyards. I sent the gun off with the police who took his body to the morgue. No, I did not want that pistol back, thank you. Watching the ambulance drive off with his body, I knew that he would miss the next chapter of the story that was leading us into a new epoch in world history. But I would not miss it. His death wiped the slate clean leaving me with my eyes wide open.

As a young Marxist, I learned about the path history was supposed to travel from feudalism to capitalism and then, inevitably, to socialism. But, it turns out, nothing is inevitable in history. I looked at the Soviet collapse from the perspective of one allied with the Soviet side of the Sino-Soviet dispute of the 1960's. I read Mao's little red book, but their Cultural Revolution left me cold. My stepfather's words echoed in my head. He said, "No man's words were gospel to me." Now, with the Soviet Union gone, and China under the rule of the triumphant Chinese Communist Party, I could see that the rise and fall of the USSR was not the whole story of Marxism. The rigid ideological battles of the past faded quickly, almost comically, after 1989, clearing the decks for a calmer approach to all the old questions.

Russell Means' challenge to Marxists entered this post Soviet opening in my thinking like flood waters after a dam collapse. Marxism posits that the working classes of industrialized nations are the main agents of progressive change. But since the working classes follow their own interests, often in conflict with people and nations outside their communities, it is hard for me to see them playing much of a progressive role. The advanced industrial and commercial economies of the US and the world provided jobs for generations of workers and molded them into groups which identified themselves with their employers and with patriotic national policies that support them. Following their own interests has led to their willingness to join imperialist armies, to scapegoat immigrants entering the US, to embrace a racially segregated society, to sanction the oppression of women and the destruction of the environment. The successful suppression of Marxism in western nations, especially the USA, reflects the supremacy of the owners of the economy and the impact of the anti-communist wars globally over the last century. Millions of workers over many generations have gone through military basic training with its patriotic orientation and absolute obedience to authority. Saluting the flag and pledging allegiance "under God" at schools and every public event has had its impact.

Under the pressures of history and European patriarchal culture, Marx's working classes are now wedded to their masters and the dictates of private property and patriarchy. These main pillars of our society reach deeply into every corner of our world and deeply into every family. The ubiquitous allegiance to "our way of life," in my view, lies behind what Means saw when he said that Europeans had proved themselves unable to hear the plea to respect nature. Restoring the Goddess and our respect for nature won't happen by decree from on high. Nor will it happen from endlessly repeating the old Marxist critique of capitalism that never mentions women nor spirituality. It can only happen when our culture lets go of patriarchy's deep roots. If Marxism is going to help in this process of transformation, it must face up to its own limitations and cease being "the same old song."

17: **Private Property and the Status of Women**

In the wake of my father's suicide, the fall of the USSR, and the rise of Communist China, I began to realize that there was a flaw inside Marxism that kept it within Europe's "same old song." Here in the USA, the mainstream continued to prattle on that communism was the loser in the great cold war that had just ended in the seeming triumph of US imperialism. Marxism was being treated with the contempt that our society loves to heap on losers. We were drunk on this arrogance as it poisoned the minds of a whole generation and a whole nation. I had ceased to pay any attention to this contempt in the 1990's along with the mainstream itself by flipping the off switch on my TV. But quietly, silently, in my mind, I continued to probe this issue wondering where Marxism's fatal flaw was located.

I was not going to join the mainstream that loves to embrace any condemnation of Marxism. No, it was like coming to grips with something in the family that had gone wrong. I had experienced the divisions and conflicts of the McCarthy period in the collapse of all the relationships of families I had grown up with. I wanted to search out this flaw in order to heal, not to injure.

I was grappling with Russell Mean's challenge to Europeans and Marxists to respect nature, and his insistence that he would not sacrifice his culture to join the class war going on in the European mainstream. I realized that class war, along with disputes like those between Adam Smith and Karl

Marx, was all within patriarchy. Understanding the ubiquity of patriarchy was like falling into a dark hole, landing on the bottom with no way out, looking up at the light wondering how to get out of this mess. The way out of this hole was to realize that patriarchy was inextricably tied to private property. Could it be that the Goddess disappeared from Marxism because, somehow, this link between private property and patriarchy was missed? I had to search more deeply into how Marxism treated the relationship between the private property and the status of women.

Friedrich Engels

I revisited Friedrich Engels' book *Origin of the Family, Private Property, and the State* to review how Engels handled the rise of private property and the fall of matrilineal cultures. I had given all my books to the Oakland Public Library some years earlier, so I had to refer to the digital version I downloaded from the web. When Engels wrote this book in 1884, he was one of the first writers seriously to examine the "gentile," i.e. female, roots of civilization. Engels examined how Greek society changed from the ancient women centered world, connecting the questions of how private property arose, to the evolution of the human family and the status of women. That was in itself a great advance in our thinking. But it was not enough.

I was startled to see that Engels envisioned the rise of private property in land, but failed to include the rise of patriarchy along with it.

The rise of private property in herds and articles of luxury led to exchange between individuals, to the transformation of products into commodities. And here lie the seeds of the whole subsequent upheaval. When the producers no longer directly consumed their product themselves, but let it pass out of their hands in the act of exchange, they lost control of it.... But the Athenians were soon to learn how rapidly the product asserts its mastery over the producer when once exchange between individuals has begun and products have been transformed into commodities. With the coming of commodity production, individuals began to cultivate the soil on their own account, which soon led to individual ownership of land.[32]

Engels uses non gendered terminology in describing this process, saying "individuals" or "producers" instead of men or women. The use of the term "men," or a non-gendered word like "producer" to refer to all humankind, pervades Engels' language leaving women and the feminine out of the discussion. This is more than semantics. Engels immersion in patriarchal culture had grave consequences for his whole analysis.

Engels asserts that the process of privatization began in pastoral areas with herds of animals.

As to how and when the herds passed out of the common possession of the tribe or the gens into the ownership of individual heads of families, we know nothing at present. . . . All the surplus which the acquisition of the necessities of life now yielded fell to the man; the woman shared in its enjoyment, but had no part in its ownership.[33]

Saying that "we know nothing" about how property "passed out of the common possession of the tribe" is not quite true. The fact is we know plenty. The rise of private property in the hands of men differs significantly from private property arising in the hands of individuals or producers who might have been either sex. We know now that 80% of the food consumed by prehistoric people came from the work of women. We also know that non patriarchal civilizations existed in the early Neolithic Era that practiced trade between far flung cultures. If early commodity production had led to the rise of ownership, i.e., cultivating the soil "on their own account," certainly women should have benefited. But they did not. The unavoidable conclusion is obvious. Private property arose in the hands of men.

The notion that the products of labor fell out of the control of "men" once the products were transformed into commodities has always been an elusive if not obscure notion to me. Products were controllable, he says, when they were traded communally inside the clan. But once "exchange between individuals has begun," they became commodities and asserted their power over the producers. Was he saying that men were mere pawns in an economic process?

When Engels failed to see gender in the rise of commodities, he turned commodities themselves into actors in the economy. Engels imputes subjective independence (the product asserting its mastery over the producer) upon an inanimate object, the commodity, which then takes control of the economy in which male rule remains hidden and unseen, or at least not mentioned.

Patriarchy hides under the rule of the commodity. No doubt it is true that men followed the market logic of commodity trading which then appears to control them. Maximizing profits became the holy grail of the new economic man. The academic field of economics arose out of making this holy grail into a universal law. Women could crash their way into this new male only club, but only after centuries of rebellion and persistence. Women remained prisoners of the household with its unpaid labor until they broke out of it. The history of these rebellions include centuries of witch burnings, rape, and cultural war that are still going on.

Engels concludes that the commodity controlled the producers without saying that this game and its rules were patriarchy in action. "Commodity controlled producers" grew out of the suppression of the Goddess. The destruction of non rational cultural values supporting our collective survival had to happen for the market to work. It despiritualizes the Earth which is no longer sacred. The Earth became a mere input into a model of economics designed to make men rich.

Why were products controllable before the rise of market economies? Was it because their distribution and consumption followed age-old traditions within cultures that did not have private property but were instead ruled by the collective sharing ethos of the Goddess oriented world? This may be an overreaching generalization, but its point is that non rational (collectivist) cultural norms of prehistory have been left out. Nineteenth century Engels sees the economy controlling behaviors of men and tries to account for that fact through the idea that commodities take on their own powers. But we know that commodities were produced and traded in the early neolithic era before patriarchal civilizations arose. What changed it? Male ownership and the inequality inherent in the class society that arose out of patriarchy.

It makes more sense to see the power of the commodity emanating from the power of the owners, who were men. The patriarchal conquest of the land and subjugation of women were the actual transformative actions of human beings in creating this new world of economic and sexual oppression.

I could see how surplus products from agriculture accelerated the rise of private property. I started with the fact that agriculture, along with sedentary village life, established itself before private property existed in the middle of the neolithic period. Before patriarchy, there was little or no incentive for individuals to sell the products of the land outside the local economies that produced them. Trade did happen but not at the scale that came later once private property arose along with its appropriation of the products into individual male hands. Early trade between different cultures began under this pre-private property way of life. There were traditional territories occupied by different cultures. There were peaceful traditions for handling interrelations between cultures which left no record of war in prehistory.

Engels' assertion that trade led to the private ownership of land may be true but it leaves out the patriarchal transformation that made trade such a powerful engine of change. Trade between matrilineal clans and cultures in prehistory set the stage for men to seize the land. Patriarchy arose as men seized the land and accelerated such pre-existing trade for their own benefit outside the matrilineal clans.

Several large conclusions followed. First, the primary act that underlies the end of prehistory and the rise of modern civilizations was men breaking from female centered cultures to seize the land or herd. This act created private property. Second, this male usurpation carried in its wake the transformation of social organization, religion, culture, language, and eventually, the earth itself. Third, it was a disaster for women. Male usurpation of the land led to the demise of the Goddess centered world globally. Male usurpation of the land made patriarchy and monogamy mandatory and became the material base of the rise of patriarchy globally. This changed human relationships to the earth with profound implications for human cultures going forward. First and foremost, it transformed the human family, a change that Engel's patriarchal bias caused him to misread.

18: Women and Monogamy

"Savagery, Barbarism and Civilization"

Engels envisioned the rise of the monogamous nuclear family unit as the result of the natural growth of economic production. Framing it in the parlance of patriarchy, he posed this transformation as the natural and inevitable rise from "savagery" to "barbarism" to "civilization." He called early human sexual relationships "promiscuity" and their cultures "savagery." In his view, these "primitive" forms evolved somehow into "group marriage" in the cultures of the next stage he called "barbarism." And then came the highest stage of the family, the "nuclear family" of "civilization."

Engels envisioned the growth of the nuclear family like a plant growing from seed, to seedling to full maturity along with the natural growth of the economy and technology. He misses the role of men in usurping the land and the consequent disastrous decline in the status of women. Instead, he asserts that the rise of civilization elevated women into the highest stage of human culture, monogamy and the nuclear family, ignoring her loss of status as she fell from Goddess to slave. Monogamy was the woman's new prison.

The rise of monogamy was not a progression from lower to higher. It was a radical transformation involving land theft and the subjugation of women. The struggle to establish male ownership of the land was accomplished through conquest. Without written records, and with the assumptions of patriarchy deeply embedded in the world around him, Engels missed the mark.

Conquests are sudden and violent like the European conquest of the Americas. History is full of reports of conquerors from Rome to Genghis Khan invading lands, capturing women and vanquishing whole cultures. Rape became standard practice of invading armies who viewed women as spoils of war. When patriarchal invaders conquered lands through violence and rape, the demise of the status women was the inevitable result.

Whether the conquerors were foreigners or not, the objective of conquest was ownership of the land. When conquest happened after invasions by foreign armies, it was common practice for the victorious empire to reward its soldiers with land grants, like Oregon did for my great grand father. In ancient times such grants might very well have fallen into the hands of the male heads of established families as a way of creating a loyal local following for the conquerors. In England, the nobility started to wear togas after being conquered by ancient Rome.

Once I understood the patriarchal character of conquest (or privatization), I could see the fundamental nature of the rise of private property as a male event within the context of the female Goddess world. Becoming a land owner transformed the men who acquired it. Patriarchy's roots dug deeply into the conquered lands as the new owners exercised their powers and wealth.

When men left the matrilineal world for patriarchy, they were now fundamentally transformed along with their relationship to the Earth and the people around them. They no longer moved into the woman's clan after marriage. Now the wives of the new property owners had to leave their mother's clan and the ancient support networks associated with them. Instead they became the prisoner of the husband who coveted his exclusive sexual access to her in order to have male heirs for his property and wealth. He no longer shared the products of the land with the whole tribe. Now, the products of the land were his alone.

Engels notes the growth of larger and larger groups of people who did not fall into the old clan groupings, including artisans, immigrants, rootless slaves, and workers who gathered in the Greek cities. These cities may have existed before patriarchy but their populations changed as private property came to dominate. Engels outlined how governing structures adapted to these new populations of slaves and migrants coming from conquered lands. These larger and larger groups outside the ancient matrilineal clans were the displaced, conquered victims of the privatization process led by men.

In the US, prehistoric cultures fell to patriarchy in the brutal suppression of tribal populations. US authorities expelled the tribes from their lands, imprisoning them onto reservations, forced them into Catholic schools where they were forbidden to speak their languages, forced to cut their hair, and exiled into cities where they fell into the bottom of a society that had no place for them. I view this American experience as a repeat of an ancient pattern that covered the globe in the spread of civilizations everywhere.

The female Goddess orientation of individuals probably remained for some time after conquest, traveling with them in their minds and hearts. As long as the female Goddess ruled the minds of the people, the control and power of the new private property owning elite faced a big problem. Greek gods, and later monotheism, arose to replace the ancient Goddess with male gods. More on that later. See Part 5 below.

19: Private Property and Gender

The right of property was the origin of evil on the earth, the first link in the long chain of crimes and misfortunes which the human race has endured since its birth.

Pierre-Joseph Proudhon, What Is Property?: or, An Inquiry into the Principle of Right and of Government

Let's conjure up the story of the first man who stole the land. His idea was to seize the land in order to capture agricultural surpluses for himself, and to end sharing with the wife's clan. If private property is theft, then men are the thieves in this first rip off. But the first theft was not necessarily a theft of land owned by others. The first man to grab a piece of land (or herd of domesticated animals) probably seized it from the mother's clan, or his wife's clan, who had been cultivating it for the tribe without holding title to it. Or it may have been a plot of land no one had been cultivating. Holding title to land is actually the result of the conquest. The concept of ownership arrived with the conquerors.

First he had to stake out his claim and fence it in. He knew how to farm it because his mothers and grandmothers had trained him to do it. This man who staked out the first plot of private property was surrounded and probably harassed by people from the mother's clan who did not like his fence. This act of seizing the land broke his ties with the traditional culture out of which he came. He might still be living with his mother's clan while at the same time laying claim to a plot of land, a farm, off in the distance. People around him might not have understood the deep significance of what he was doing. Before his seizure of the land, all his hard work on that farm created wealth that kept merging into the clan's traditional ways of appropriation and distribution. Once he asserted his ownership, he faced the prospect of doing without the communal labor of his tribe or clan who were now excluded from the harvest. Slavery arose to provide the new owner with labor so he could begin to accumulate wealth for himself alone. (See James c. Scott's *Against the Grain* for an idea of the complexity and impact of this transition.)

After a life on a privately owned farm, and in order to solidify his hold on the land, he had to arrange to give this land and its production to his son to continue his name and accumulate more wealth. Leaving it to his daughter would likely have put it back into the hands of a woman who was still untamed by patriarchal domination and close to the matrilineal clans surrounding him. Leaving it to a daughter would merge it back into the old world. Without written records, but with the world today as we know it, it is not far-fetched to assert that this privatization process was happening in many places at once and was repeating itself generation after generation. It spread by example. But even more, it spread by conquest from the outside.

The spread of patriarchal cultures through conquest accelerated the process everywhere. Just like our well documented conquest of North America, the spread of private property and patriarchy transformed cultures and lands from one end of the Earth to the other. It spread over the millenniums and created both abundance and conflict wherever it went. Marija Gimbutas identifies the Indo-European invasions as just such an event.

Civilizations arose in this complex process of privatization, along with the rise of privileged classes of nobles, the expansion of trade and the political conflict that followed it inevitably. As the amount of land claimed privately expanded, traditional cultures were pushed into the margins or destroyed completely through violence. Prehistoric abundance created by peace loving societies within the traditional world was a plum to be easily picked, just like taking a plum from a tree that does not defend against the picking of its fruit.

As small enclaves of civilization arose, surviving groups of traditional people were transformed from matrilineal independent cultures to become patriarchal dominated suppliers of raw materials, people and crafts for the great estates and the cities. These outlying groups have come to be known as barbarians. Peaceful tribes of the ancient world were required to take up warfare in order to survive and preserve their way of life.

This male-led transformation brought about many astounding new developments, like writing to keep track of the estates and science to preserve ancient knowledge in a new form supporting private owners. In this way the fruits of ancient knowledge were transformed into tools for the advancement of patriarchy and private property.

However, ancient knowledge did not transfer easily into the new male property owning society. Much of it was lost at the same time that it became the basis of modern science. Practitioners of science in the old world were in demand in the new world. But now science no longer benefited the whole tribe. Its new role was as a servant of private property.

The Midwife

The nature of the transition to patriarchy can be seen when we consider the transformation of the role of the midwife. The midwife of the ancient world arose to insure the survival of our species. Midwives operated within the female centered social world freely and were honored and respected for their role in helping women give birth. The midwife in the new patriarchal world threatened male control of the wife and offspring through the reassertion of the independence and autonomy of the women centered world within a patriarchal household. The midwife was both needed and rejected, leaving mothers to suffer the consequences.

Ancient knowledge before private property was an asset for guiding the whole people to live in harmony with nature and to insure the survival of humanity and all life. In the hands of private property, ancient knowledge boiled down to a tool for making greater wealth and power for a man at the expense of the rest of life and the planet. Science still suffers from this diminished role today. As the ancients passed away, a vast body of knowledge went underground living on with the slaves and displaced people of the mother clans. This underground knowledge resurfaced in the modern era when people like Marija Gimbutas made the connection between the symbols of popular culture in the Lithuania of her youth and the meaning of the ancient symbols she unearthed in her archaeological digs.

20: Culture and Conquest

Matrilineal clans formed the basic cultural context within which men seized the land. People raised children inside homes and villages with their mothers, and their mother's relatives, brothers, uncles, grandmothers, grandfathers, aunts, cousins, etc. When boys came of age and married, they most often moved away into the wife's clan. As long as a man behaved himself, he lived with her. If he did not behave himself, he got sent home to his mother's clan. Labeling ancient sexual relationships as promiscuity appealed to the patriarchs mainly because they did not rule over it.

It wasn't just the women who sent misbehaving men home. It was also the men of her clan. Men and women adhered to the values handed down over the years. Monogamy was just not happening. This did not mean that men were subordinated to women. It just meant that this is how life was ordered within ancient cultures. Prehistoric women were esteemed and even worshiped, occupying a much higher status than today. Men contributed in many ways, including tribal leadership, hunting, sharing wisdom in passing down oral traditions, helping to raise children, and doing some of the heavy work.

Fundamental Contradictions

Without private property, there were no fundamental contradictions between people. The earth provides enough for all life. Wisdom of the ancients, gained over tens of thousands of years, guided human kind to keep it that way.

I believe that this prehistoric way of life is the non settler origins of my ancestors I had been searching for. Our identity as a species (aka, human nature) arose from these origins that lasted thousands of years. It may appear to be a far distant reality, irrelevant today. But it also defines human nature far better than the definitions that have arisen during the era of patriarchy. Our ancient roots provide us with an anchor for thinking about how to move forward towards finding a sustainable way of life.

Other writers have taken this insight much further than anything I could even imagine. Tyson Yunkaporta's insightful book *Sand Talk: How Indigenous Thinking Can Save the World* actually applies traditional knowledge of Australian aborigines to modern settler ways with suggestions of how to fix the mess we have created. Yunkaporta demonstrated to me how the destructive interaction between settlers and indigenous people is global in scope. He gave me a deeper understanding of the insights in Marija Gimbutas studies of European prehistory.

Marija Gimbutas

Marija Gimbutas focused on the Indo-European invasions' impact on the societies of Old Europe.

> *The Indo-European incursions into central Europe, from the late fifth to the early third millennia B.C., caused a linguistic and cultural discontinuity.*

These incursions disrupted the Old European sedentary farming lifestyle that had existed for three thousand years. As the Indo-European tribes encroached on Old Europe from the east, the continent underwent upheavals. These severely affected the Balkans, where the Old European cultures abundantly employed script. The Old European way of life deteriorated rapidly, although pockets of Old European culture remained for several millennia. The new peoples spoke completely different languages belonging to the Indo-European linguistic family. The Old European language or languages, and the script used to write them, declined and eventually vanished from central Europe.[34]

Her description of the impact of Indo-European invasions of Europe on the Old European language and cultures matches the impact of the European invasion of the Americas. There were patriarchal civilizations in the Americas that arose indigenously (Incas, Mayans, Aztecs) at the time of the European "discovery". The impact of the conquest was the same for them. The conquests were all about land seizure and anyone who stood in the way was obliterated. This prehistoric transition brought an end to the peaceful millennia of prehistory.

Gimbutas characterizes the transition to the warfare state:

It is a gross misunderstanding to imagine warfare as endemic to the human condition. Widespread fighting and fortification building have indeed been the way of life for most of our direct ancestors from the Bronze Age up until now. However, this was not the case in the Paleolithic and Neolithic. There are no depictions of arms (weapons used against other humans) in Paleolithic cave paintings, nor are there remains of weapons used by man against man during the Neolithic of Old Europe. From some hundred and fifty paintings that survived at Catal Huytik, there is not one depicting a scene of conflict or fighting, or of war or torture.[35]

The literature and controversies about our female origins is vast and continues to grow in academia and beyond. Current attempts, mostly by women writers, to bring gender into the study of archaeology has acted like a vanguard assault on the patriarchal bias that permeates the world today.

Some women writers, like Sjöö and Mor, Marija Gimbutas, Merlin Stone, Sarah Milledge Nelson and others, have put together enough scholarship to allow us to gaze upon this matrilineal prehistory and begin to think about what it means. Their writings are enough for me to accept their characterization of prehistory. The destruction of the original female centered civilizations, along with outlaying nomadic cultures, is the basic context for the destructive impact we continue to have on indigenous cultures and the natural world.

Patriarchal civilization developed religious blinders against these female roots that are now built into modern patriarchal cultures, our educational institutions and churches. Cultural blindness to prehistory follows largely from the influence of sacred biblical and philosophical texts handed down to us over countless generations. When I look at

Black Elk's dream, with the sacred woman, the council of grandfathers and the flowering tree at the center of the circle, I see a philosophy of life in harmony with nature. Similarly, I see that the religious and philosophical cannons of our society blinds us to nature and binds us to environmental destruction, warfare, racism and misogamy.

My new understanding of the end of prehistory made me wonder about Greek mythology. How did the ancient philosophers of patriarchy see the origins of their way of life? Maybe I could see the outlines of the demise of the Goddess somewhere in their writings. After all, these writers were thousands of years closer to the times when the Goddess was universally respected than we are today. I began to dig into the myths like an archaeologist in a graveyard.

Private Property and the Goddess

Part 5: Greek Myths

I understand Greek myths as poetic expressions of how human consciousness adapted to the world after the suppression of the Goddess. Humanity faced a Void, an emptiness, that had never existed before they left their tribal homes to wander the streets of the new patriarchal owned lands. With powerful new land owners calling the shots, humanity still lived in a spiritual world that demanded a new theological order for what was emerging. Over the centuries and millennia, a vast variety of local Greek traditions arose that told how the new gods came to be and how they established permanent control over the cosmos.

I started out reading Hesiod's *Theogony* which synthesized these oral traditions that went back 2500 years before he wrote his book sometime around 700 BC, two hundred years before the Bible appeared. I found Hesiod's poetic story laced with symbolic meaning that elevated it from a story of events into a story of spiritual transformation as the new world emerged. It is the story of the new ruling class' way of seeing the world.

21: The Myths Hide Prehistory

The Abyss

Greek mythology and the Bible both start out with the Void or the Abyss. At first, they say, there was nothing. Then all these things happened. How, I wondered, did people come to accept such an improbable notion as the Void? Belief in such an idea grew along with the wars to seize the land that happened during the last half of the Neolithic Era. The ancient wars of conquest shaped the psyche of ancient times in the same way that basic training in the military today shapes the psyche of modern times. A peace loving individual is transformed when he finds himself with a weapon in his hands facing the choice to kill or be killed. Survival mode kicks in and one's ideas follow behind it.

The concept of the Abyss was part of the war against the Goddess. Is it any different than our modern propaganda, I wondered? How can we understand the war in Vietnam, for instance, if we think of the Vietnamese as "gooks?" Such concepts reduce real humans to unworthy enemies instead of people who were fighting for their independence and freedom. For the Greeks, the abyss erases the universal Goddess who was being obliterated through land seizures. Conquerors reduce their victims to inhuman status reserved for "enemies" everywhere. The lasting impact of this process is visible in the widespread ignorance and contempt for so-called "primitive" people that permeates modern civilization.

Edith Hamilton's Prehistory

Edith Hamilton's 1942 book *Mythology, Timeless Tales of Gods and Heros*, gives expression to this distorted view of prehistory that is still in vogue today.

> *Nothing is clearer than the fact that primitive man, whether in New Guinea today or eons ago in the prehistoric wilderness, is not and never has been a creature who peoples his world with bright fancies and lovely visions. Horrors lurked in the primeval forest, not nymphs and naiads. Terror lived there, with its close attendant, Magic, and its most common defense, Human Sacrifice.*[36]

For Edith Hamilton, prehistory was full of terror and cannibalism for "primitive man." She does not identify prehistory with our female origins. Instead, patriarchal assumptions permeate her low opinion of scary prehistory.

> *Of course the Greeks too had their roots in the primeval slime. Of course they too once lived a savage life, ugly and brutal. But what the myths show is how high they had risen above the ancient filth and fierceness by the time we have any knowledge of them. Only a few traces of that time are to be found in the stories... The tales of Greek mythology do not throw any clear light upon what early mankind was like. They do throw an abundance of light upon what early Greeks were like—a matter, it would seem, of more importance to us, who are their descendants intellectually, artistically, and politically, too.*[37]

Slime, filth, ugly, brutal, savage, fierceness dominated her view of prehistory. Averting her eyes from a darkness of her own making, she embraces the idealism of the myths as her salvation.

> *With the coming forward of Greece, mankind became the center of the universe, the most important thing in it. This was a revolution in thought. Human beings had counted for little heretofore. In Greece man first realized what mankind was.*
>
> *The Greeks made their gods in their own image. That had not entered the mind of man before. Until then, gods had had no semblance of reality. . . . The early Greek mythologists transformed a world full of fear into a world full of beauty.*[38]

This "revolution in thought" had indeed "entered the mind of man." Contrary to Hamilton's assertion that "the tales of Greek mythology do not throw any clear light upon what early mankind was like", I was surprised to discover that shining the light of our female origins onto the ancient myths revealed quite a lot about the transition from the Goddess to the gods of Mount Olympus.

22: The Abyss and Primordial Gods

Hesiod

Hesiod's story starts with the myth chronicler asking the Muses, six daughters of Zeus, to tell the story of the gods. Hesiod's story unfolds as told by the fourth generation of immortal Greek gods to a mere mortal male writer of tales. Kind of like Walter Cronkite interviews Moses on the mountain.

> *Tell how [the writer asks the Muses] first the gods and*
>   *earth came into being*
> *And the rivers and the sea, endless and surging,*
> *And the stars shining and the wide sky above;*
> *How they divided wealth and allotted honors,*
> *And first possessed deep-ridged Olympos.*[39]

Hesiod's narrator includes two questions about the origins of the first gods: "how they divided wealth" and "first possessed deep-ridged Olympos." Right from the start, the ancient myths tell us how wealth and property ownership derived from the gods. The initial focus on inequality and private property claim their place at the top of the origins story. These two questions reveal the nature of the Goddess world without gross inequality and land ownership.

The Muses answer:

> *In the beginning there was only Chaos, the Abyss,*
> *But then Gaia, the Earth, came into being,*
> *Her broad bosom the ever-firm foundation of all,*
> *And Tartaros, dim in the underground depths,*
> *And Eros, loveliest of all the Immortals, who*
> *Makes their bodies (and men's bodies) go limp,*
> *Mastering their minds and subduing their wills.*

> *From the Abyss were born Erebos and dark Night.*
> *And Night, pregnant after sweet intercourse*
> *With Erebos, gave birth to Aether and Day.*
>
> *Earth's first child was Ouranos, starry Heaven,*
> *Just her size, a perfect fit on all sides,*
> *And a firm foundation for the blessed gods.*
> *And she bore the Mountains in long ranges, haunted*
> *By the Nymphs who live in the deep mountain dells.*
> *Then she gave birth to the barren, raging Sea*
> *Without any sexual love.*[40]

Both male and female primordial gods appeared out of the Abyss. These primordial gods were setting up the context for the conflict to come between the Goddess and the new patriarchs, or put another way, the struggle to assert male ownership. Having both genders among the primordial gods contrasts sharply with the Biblical myth that followed centuries later starting out with its all male God alone in the sky, removing the female from the heavens entirely. Not so with the Greeks who were much closer to the prehistoric Goddess.

Out of the Abyss emerge the basic patriarchal components of the universe, according to Hesiod. First there was the female earth (Gaia), then male hell (Tartaros), then male Eros (love), then female darkness (Nyx) and her brother (Erebos), the personification of darkness. Heaven is born (without a father) from the earth. Light and Day are born after darkness (Nyx) mates with her brother, Erebos. Then Earth gives birth to the mountains and the barren sea "without sexual love."

Once earth gives birth to the heavens, Ouranos, she takes him as her husband and procreation proceeds.

Ouranos is her son and then her husband. Earth gives birth to the Titans and the Cyclops. Then Gaia and Ouranos produce the other Olympians. Gaia remains the first and primary deity associated with earth, death and the Underworld. Clearly, Gaia in the Greek world is the descendant of the Goddess now coexisting with other male and female elements.

When the primordial gods cede their powers to their descendants, like the property owner must when he dies, a struggle to rule over Gaia begins between Ouranos and his male offspring.

Off the top, I had to wonder what happened to the incest taboo? All the gods derive from sexual unions between mother and son. Then, all these gods proceed to marry their brothers and sisters. The incest taboo clearly did not apply to the gods. The gods lived in a different world from mortals who were bound by the incest taboo handed down from ancient times. Now the new gods occupied a superior position where the rules of society did not apply. If I were to guess, I might say that the first property owners had a hard time finding a bride and had to resort to sex within their own families. It also seems to legitimize predatory sexual behavior of mortal men.

New Gods and the Land

These new gods were to rule the minds of Greek civilization for centuries and millenniums to come. These new patriarchal gods spread to the rest of the world, along with the spread of private ownership of the land. Owners most likely believed in their hearts that the gods demanded their actions. A new god of land ownership appeared early in the Greek creation story as Plutus, the son of Demeter, Zeus' sister and goddess of the harvest. (See below, "27: The Goddess Refused to Die" for Demeter's story).

In Marija Gimbutas' framework of humanity as spiritual beings, the new land owners might have called on Plutus to show them the way. Such moments of religious epiphany might then be sanctified and validated by his group as they became aware of his vision and power in building this new way of life.

Once the new gods were invoked, other men and women might believe and profess loyalty to them. These sky god worshipers at first might have appeared as cults living in little groups here and there. The sky god believers probably started out small in number and then grew larger and more numerous as time passed. The first two generations of Greek gods appear to represent this period of transition when the new myths spread during the thousands of years before Hesiod and Homer finally wrote their story down.

Black Elks' dream provided me with a mirror image of how the new gods took root among the captured and displaced people. The four ascents Black Elk traveled in his dream identify how the circle of the people was broken and what happened to the tribe as they were defeated and oppressed. The physical decline through war, disease, hunger, and oppression knocked the traditional divinities down. The people were no longer cared for and nurtured by the circle of the people. They suffered as they saw the world change. Those who survived were none the less spiritual as they lived through this decline, finding new ways of surviving. The appeal of the oppressors' gods becomes the appeal of adapting to a new form of life imposed upon them from outside. The spiritual nature of the Earth, central to the old ways, dims in their minds and hearts as slave and wage labor is imposed upon them. In his reservation years, after Wounded Knee, Black Elk joined the Jesuits to share in this transformation which he and his people were going through.

In prehistoric times, new male landowners must have seen the limitless potential for the accumulation of wealth that domesticated agriculture combined with trade offered them. Attaching this earthly vision to new male gods spreads along with the power and wealth of the new land owners. This new vision of the middle neolithic period seems to have let a genie out of the bottle, accompanied by Pandora's jar of miseries and false hope, that spread like wildfire, transforming cultures everywhere.

23: The First Rebellion: Castrating Father Sky

Patriarchy's War

Ouranos emerged from Gaia as her son and then her husband. The Earth gave birth to the heavens. Then they married. For Gaia to give birth to Ouranos and then accept him as her husband is a portrayal of the transition to patriarchy. A male god rises as a child of the Earth to become her ruler in one step. The marriage of the Earth and the heavens was shaky from the start. The heavens distrusted their offspring. The marriage gave the heavens dominion over the Earth but could not break the children's loyalty to their mother. The children did not accept the sky gods powers. The sky god then rejected the children by stuffing them back into the Earth. This sets up the stage for the first rebellion: the castration of father sky.

In the lead up to the rebellion, Gaia gave birth to the twelve Titans, six males and six females. The females did not come from a man's rib, but from Gaia herself, and stood independently on their own feet. Women standing on their own feet was a concept the pre-civilized world knew well.

The last Titan to be born was Cronus (also spelled Cronos):

> *...a most terrible child,*
> *Cronos, her youngest, an arch-deceiver,*
> *And this boy hated his lecherous father.*[41]

Gaia and Ouranos also became parents of the Cyclops with their lone eye in the middle of their foreheads and of the hundred-handers, "strong hulking creatures that beggar description."

> *A hundred hands stuck out of their shoulders,*
> *Grotesque, and fifty heads grew on each stumpy neck.*
> *These monsters exuded irresistible strength.*
> *They were Gaia's most dreaded offspring,*
> *And from the start their father feared and loathed them.*
> *Ouranos used to stuff all of his children*
> *Back into a hollow of Earth soon as they were born,*
> *Keeping them from the light, an awful thing to do,*
> *But Heaven did it, and was very pleased with*
> *himself.*
>
> *Vast Earth groaned under the pressure inside,*
> *And then she came up with a plan, a really wicked*
> *trick.*
> *She created a new mineral, gray flint, and formed*
> *A huge sickle from it and showed it to her dear boys.*
> *And she rallied them with this bitter speech:*
>
> *"Listen to me, children, and we might yet get even*
> *With your criminal father for what he has done to us.*
> *After all, he started this whole ugly business." [said*
> *Gaia.]*
> *"I think I might be able to bring it off, Mother, [replied*
> *Cronus.]*
> *"I can't stand Father; he doesn't even deserve the name.*
> *And after all, he started this whole ugly business."*
> *This response warmed the heart of vast Earth.*

With Gaia's help, Cronus takes revenge against Ouranos to the cheers of the "vast Earth." Gaia created a scythe made out of stone (flint) which Cronus then used to castrate Ouranos.

> *She hid young Cronos in an ambush and placed in his*
> *   hands*
> *The jagged sickle.*
> *Then she went over the whole plan with him.*
> *And now on came great Ouranos, bringing Night with*
> *   him.*
> *And, longing for love, he settled himself all over Earth.*
> *From his dark hiding-place, the son reached out*
> *With his left hand, while with his right he swung*
> *The fiendishly long and jagged sickle, pruning the*
> *   genitals*
> *Of his own father with one swoop and tossing them*
> *Behind him, where they fell to no small effect.*
> *Earth soaked up all the bloody drops that spurted out.*[42]

Having her son castrate her husband is certainly a sign of a marriage gone bad. They had some serious differences. Yes, Ouranos stuffed his children back into Gaia. Yes, he thought Gaia's offspring were ugly. But was that it? Was that enough to account for this deep hostility? I had to put it into the context of the historical fight over the land which at first went badly for the new patriarchs.

I had to realize that the point of the new myths was first and foremost to justify replacing the mother right, "the custom by which dynastic succession passes only in the female line," with patriarchy. By the time the myths were written, patriarchal property ownership was well established. Many Goddess cultures had been destroyed or pushed into the hills. Gaia's intent was to preserve the mother right. Ouranos's intent was to end it. Gaia's son/husband Ouranos goes to war against all their offspring in order to preserve his claim to the land. He put all the Titans in Tartaros. Castration certainly cut that part of the story short and Cronus takes over.

Ouranos blamed his hatred on the children because he thought they were so horrible. He found the hundred handers and the cyclops repulsive. His repulsion about his own children then motivated him to stuff them back into the Earth. Imagining Gaia's offspring as horrible and repulsive brought to my mind the racial stereotypes that American slave owners put on black slaves, some of whom were their own children. Sambo could easily have been a reincarnation of the cyclops and served the same purpose of justifying the oppressive behavior of the new masters. Attributing Ouranos behavior in stuffing his offspring back into Gaia to their repulsiveness is the slave owners' version of this story.

Looking at it from the woman's side, below the heavenly framework of the myths, I asked myself what Ouranos' repulsion says about the early conflicts resulting from the male appropriation of the land? It says to me that the father and son got into a power struggle from the start. Loyalty to the mother stood in the way. Cronus was Gaia's tool used to wrestle control away from Ouranos and save her children. Her efforts threatened to reassert the mother right over the farm. Male appropriation of the land had to keep the land under male control. That was the real source of his repulsion and his war against his children. He had to break their loyalty to their mother and her clan.

The struggle between Ouranos and Gaia emerged soon after the gods took possession of Mount Olympus. It incorporates the dilemmas that mortal men must have encountered when they first began raising a family on a plot of land outside the support structures of ancient female centered village. Moving to a privately owned farm would require the woman to sacrifice her place in the circle of women at the center of prehistoric cultures and all the age-old customs that supported her. It sounds like a bad deal. She and her children would have been all too aware of the alternative life with the mother's clan. She might have chosen to leave the farm and go back to mom, leaving the guy to stew in his own juices back on his precious little plot of land. And indeed, the history of all early empires contain repeated accounts of work forces running off back to the hills leaving the crops to die. Some have speculated that the Great Wall of China was built to keep slave laborers in as much as it was to keep the Mongol hordes out.

To make patriarchy work, he could not permit such escapes and rebellions. Getting rid of the kids was one alternative. Another alternative would be to declare (holy) war on the prehistoric tribes so she had nowhere else to go. Evidently, Ouranos could not work it out. It was up to the next generation to carry on the fight.

So, back on Mount Olympus, Cronus, the youngest Titan, took over. After he castrated Ouranos and becomes the new King, he began his reign by freeing his brothers and sisters, the Titans, from Tartaros where Ouranos had put them. Cronus disabled the Cyclops and hundred handers who were guarding them. It is no coincidence that it was not the eldest son who did this since he was probably running around in the hills with his tribe.

With Cronus in charge, his freed siblings pledged their loyalties to their mother and rejected the father. But Cronus still had a problem even with Ouranos' genitals floating in the sea.

Aphrodite

Castrating Ouranos, the first act of rebellion, gave rise to the antithesis of the Goddess in the form of Aphrodite who was to be ruled by the male primordial god Eros. Aphrodite arose to give women an ideal to follow living under the rule of men and an alternative to escaping back to mom's clan.

> *The genitalia themselves, freshly cut with flint, were thrown*
> *Clear of the mainland into the restless, white-capped sea,*
> *Where they floated a long time. A white foam from the god-flesh*
> *Collected around them, and in that foam a maiden developed*
> *And grew.... She came ashore, an awesome, beautiful divinity.*
> *Tender grass sprouted up under her slender feet. Aphrodite.*
> *She loves the organs of sex, from which she made her epiphany.*
> *Eros became her companion, and ravishing Desire waited on her*

> *At her birth and when she made her debut among the*
>   *Immortals.*
> *From that moment on, among both gods and humans,*
> *She has fulfilled the honored function that includes*
> *Virginal sweet-talk, lovers' smiles and deceits,*
> *And all of the gentle pleasures of sex.*[43]

As beautiful and desirable as she was, the emergence of Aphrodite was a major demotion. Women fell from universal Goddess, worshiped as the source of all life, to the one dimensional sex slave who "loves the organs of sex." She emerged from the earthly white ocean foam bubbling up around the castrated genitals of Ouranos, not from the female womb, but from the imagination of a man.

Aphrodite, says the myths, owes her existence to Ouranos' godly genitals, which occasioned her epiphany in the world. It is easy to imagine this notion originating in the plight of the first men to seize the land. He has rebelled against the Goddess culture and laid a claim to the land for himself alone. He is having a hard time finding a wife who will give him some male children to leave the property to when the time comes. Ancient custom had placed the control of children in women's hands. They believed that children come from the spirits and ancestors, not from the father.

So imagine this man, outside the confines of the cultures that raised him, needing a wife. He couldn't just barge into the circle of women, point to one, and say, "Ok, you, come with me and I will take charge of the children that we create." The woman might laugh. "Oh really, you will raise the kids? Ha!" The man replies, "No, my dear, you will do it but I will rule over you." The whole clan centered around the woman would not go for it at all. They would throw him out and slam the door. His only alternative would be to use force. To grab her and lock her up in his little farm house.

But, if he raided the village and grabbed her, she could run off back to the village the first time he turned his back. So feeling alone and rejected, laying there in his farm house, he imagines the ideal woman. He needs her for sex and procreation. So the ideal would be a woman who "loves the organs of sex." She would be beautiful and young and charming. And she would believe in him and his power over the land. He would call her Aphrodite!

How does Cronus' act of castrating Ouranos fit into this early patriarchal scene? I look at Gaia, not as the Goddess, but as a stand-in for the first woman who left the mother's clan for the tiny farm house on the "privatized" land. By doing so, this first woman left the ancient Goddess for Ouranos, the father god in the sky. But inside her, in her body, she brings the real Goddess along with her into the patriarchal center. They have a bunch of kids, but Ouranos distrusts them and gets rid of them. The new wife finally rebels with the help of the youngest (and last) child, Cronus.

Her rebellion against Ouranos, sky god, was Gaia's last stand in the face of male supremacy. She wasn't asserting the primacy of the Goddess over the Greek's pantheon of male gods. She wasn't asking for a divorce, nor was she trying to kill him. She just wanted to stop him from killing the children. She couldn't make him trust them, not with the mother's clan looming large as a really great alternative just over the hill.

So she joins up with Cronus and they decide to stop any more kids from being born. To do this, she draws from the storehouse of prehistoric tools and hands Cronus the flint scythe to do the deed. The myths arose in the bronze age when empires ruled with new weapons created out of bronze. The surrounding woman-centered clans still used flint. Thus, the rebellion of the prehistoric cultures is embodied in the myths with this use of the ancient tool to castrate Ouranos.

Cronus figures it's his turn to make a go of it, and so shacks up with his sister Rhea to make more kids. Cronus continues in his father's footsteps with his incestuous marriage, not with his mother, but this time, with his sister. He is no more able to trust his kids than Ouranos was able to trust Cronus. Instead of putting them back into the earth, he swallows them, putting them into his body. He may have just thought he would hold on to them for later.

As men seized the land, they sought divine sanction for their act of theft. They sought divine sanction for their rule over women in a world centered around and run by women. The act of faith in joining father sky, instead of continuing to worship Mother Earth, is fundamental to the viability of life in the little farm house. The males had to know the power of this faith to shape the future of the farm. The only way forward was to cultivate this new faith in the woman to keep her subdued and make her forget the alternatives. The key to the future of patriarchy was her loyalty to the father god in the sky.

Patriarchy's ascent led to the fundamental change in the status of women as she descended into slavery and monogamy. Piece by piece, the new heavenly father tore away the elements of the universe from the mother goddess and placed them into the conceptual framework of the male dominated world.

Trouble and Strife

Displaced people coming to the towns and villages growing up around the new plantations were cast into a world of trouble and strife. So it is logical and unsurprising that chief among the new gods was Eris, the goddess of strife, discord, contention and rivalry.

> *These goddesses never let up their dread anger*
> *Until the sinner has paid a severe penalty.*
> *And deadly Night bore Nemesis too, more misery*
> *For mortals; and after her, Deception and Friendship*
> *And ruinous Old Age, and hard-hearted Eris.*
> *And hateful Eris bore agonizing Toil,*
> *Forgetfulness, Famine, and tearful Pains,*
> *Battles and Fights, Murders and Manslaughters,*
> *Quarrels, Lying Words, and Words Disputations,*
> *Lawlessness and Recklessness, who share one nature,*
> *And Oath, who most troubles men upon Earth*
> *When anyone willfully swears a false oath.*[44]

Patriarchy puts a new Olympian goddess in charge of the heavenly forces that bring woes into everyone's lives. Eris now heaps "Toil, Forgetfulness, Famine, and tearful Pains, Battles and Fights..." on the beleaguered masses now wandering rootless among the new powerful estates. Including forgetfulness in the list of curses on mortals gave holy sanction to patriarchy's need to wipe the Goddess from the minds of the slaves and displaced. The notion of the Abyss covered over the details of the transition from the Goddess to the sky gods.

24: Cronus Takes Over

Gaia's plan works like a charm. Once castrated, Ouranos is pushed aside. Cronus takes over and his reign as king begins. But with Eris stirring the pot, Cronus has troubles at every turn. First, he owes his throne to his mother, Gaia. Next, he marries his sister Rhea and they have children.

Cronus and Rhea's children prove to be no more trustworthy than Cronus had. Cronus distrust of his children causes him to swallow them instead of following his father's example of stuffing them back into the Earth. A not-so-subtle change occurs as the children go into the male's body instead of back to Gaia, the female's body. The battlefield had shifted. Gaia fades further into the background as Rhea, emulating Gaia, now fights Cronus for her children's survival. Rhea, just like Gaia, becomes an ally of her youngest son, Zeus.

These first two generations of Greek gods, Ouranos and Cronus, were both afflicted by the continuing influence of women, Gaia and her daughter Rhea. This period of uncertainty and struggle might well reflect the struggle of early landowners to establish and maintain their exclusive rights over the land while being surrounded by the Goddess cultures of prehistory.

Gaia was the main instigator of the first rebellion. Once Cronus succeeds in castrating his father and assuming the throne, he remains in a precarious situation fearing his children just like Ouranos had feared his (and for good reason). The myth shifts away from Gaia who recedes from power along with Ouranos. They predict that Cronus will be overthrown by his own children. Cronus frees the Titans (his brothers) and together they rule the cosmos. But Rhea does not like all her children being swallowed up by her brother/husband. So she hides the youngest, Zeus.

25: Zeus Rules the Third Generation

The contentious story of buried and swallowed children, and fighting between fathers and sons, had to resolve itself sooner or later. Patriarchy required absolute rule and supreme power. Zeus accomplished this goal. The story of Zeus' rise to power in a struggle against his father, Cronus, started with Rhea's anger at Cronus for swallowing their children. When her belly was swollen with Zeus, the story goes, she fled to Crete, the last stronghold of the Goddess world, where she gave birth to Zeus in a cave on Mount Dicte and raised him in secret. Rhea wrapped a stone in swaddling clothes and gave it to Cronus to swallow as if it were their newborn child.

In the myths, Cronus fought a war against Ouranos with the help of the Titans whom Ouranos had buried in the earth in Tartaros. Cronus freed the Titans and allied with them to achieve victory over Ouranos. When Zeus went to war with Cronus and his Titans, Zeus allied himself with the remaining inhabitants in Tartaros. They defeated Cronus and the Titans whom Zeus threw back into Tartaros. This sequence suggests the victory of patriarchy and the origins of war. In the process, it should be noted, Zeus released the inhabitants of hell onto the Earth.

Rhea faced the basic conflict confronting all women in the transition to patriarchy. The practice of killing or exiling unwanted children is not unfamiliar in ancient tales of all sorts. As women sank deeper into patriarchal captivity, they faced a new competition for the loyalty of the children, and sometimes, for the very lives of their children. If patriarchs killed "disloyal" children, including girl babies, rather than giving them a share or letting them return to the tribe, a mother was left powerless and alone without her children. A real alternative to this powerlessness was to ally with one man over others as suited her best interests. Zeus' rise to power in the myth goes like this:

> *When Zeus became an adult, he took his niece Metis, daughter of his brother, Oceanos, as his accomplice, and she gave Cronus a drug to swallow. Under its influence he was forced first to vomit up the stone, then the children that he had swallowed. Together with these regurgitated offspring, Zeus fought the war against Cronus and the Titans. They had been fighting for ten years when Ge [Gaia] foretold that Zeus would be victorious if he took as allies those who had been thrown into Tartaros. . . . He killed Campe, who guarded them, and loosed their bindings. And then the Cyclopes gave Zeus thunder, lightning, and the thunderbolt; they gave Hades a helmet; and they gave Poseidon a trident. Armed with these weapons, they defeated the Titans, threw them into Tartaros and set the Hundred-Handers to guard them. As for themselves, they cast lots for dominion, and Zeus received power in the sky, Poseidon power in the sea, and Plouton power in the house of Hades.*[45]

Patriarchy wins the war through recruiting its army from the inhabitants of hell. Zeus could be victorious, Gaia predicted, if he allied himself with the inhabitants of Tartaros. This alliance was a new turn of events. Instead of allying himself with the previously untrustworthy Titan gods who were defending Cronus, he allied himself with the dispossessed, the losers who had been sent to Tartaros. Rhea knew which way the wind was blowing and clued Zeus in. His allies in the struggle for power were the victims of the patriarchal dictatorship. Joining the army of the empire was a sure path to upward mobility for them. And it remains so today.

Zeus received his powers (thunder, lightning and the thunderbolt) from the Cyclops, who were born from the union of the Gaia and Ouranos, or earth and heaven. Handing down these powers establishes the continuity between the world of the Goddess and Zeus. He inherits the powers of the old world who came out of the Abyss. He now achieves total dominance, allowing him to draw straws to decide which part of the earth he and his brothers will rule.

So the story unfolds. Women could gain power only through the male gods. The experiences of war created new loyalties to Zeus and launched the powers of the new age.

26: From Goddess to Slave

During this transitional beginning, the status of women in society fell from her preeminence as an expression of the Goddess forces of creation to subjugation as a wife and slave of the land owner. Women were captured in wars, starved and raped into accepting their new situation. And over time and generations, some women came to accept the new patriarchal gods. The time frame of this decline probably spanned from 12,000 BC with the origin of private property, continuing through 1,500 BC when plowed fields had engulfed the Stonehenge complex in England, showing that it had lost its sacred functions to private land owning farmers.

Along with access to their traditional lands, women lost their sexual freedom and the family security that non-owning collective cultures had provided. Now, women were confined in monogamous families and subject to the male's power. In the Goddess Era, sexuality existed without monogamy. To western thinkers, including Frederick Engels, it was seen as promiscuity (having or characterized by many transient sexual relationships). To see non-monogamous sexuality as promiscuous is a male projection based on the monogamous ideal. Promiscuity seems to be the only way a patriarchal man of civilization could understand sexual relationships outside his power.

Pre-patriarchal, non-monogamous sexual relations had existed for tens of thousands of years giving rise to millions of human beings and countless cultures living in peace with each other all over the world.

There is no reason to believe that prehistoric sexual relations were transient or necessarily frequent. They were based on age-old traditions in each culture centered in the maternal clan. Since children were cared for in the maternal circles of prehistoric societies, the paternity of the child did not matter. The father's role in raising children was shared with all the males in the mother's clan which the biological father joined with the consent of the woman. It was a different way of life, not chaos. Its great sin was that it did not include patriarchal private ownership of the land or women.

Once the mother's clan was vanquished, sexuality became a threat to male supremacy, to his ownership of the land in the male line. Patriarchy had to secure the ownership of the woman herself, to give her his name, to restrict her sexual relations to himself alone, to remove her entirely from her mother's clan. And yet he had no choice but to entrust his children to this new slave/wife.

Captured women likely became the foundation for the institution of slavery in ancient human history. The male owner tied his wife to himself through religion and force–the same force used to seize the land. As we know, women's work provided 80% of the sustenance for the whole tribe in prehistory. Owning a woman was fundamental to owning the labor needed to grow crops. Slavery also ensured worker's inferior legal status and ended their ancient habits of living freely on the earth.

Patriarchy acted like a wrecking ball on cultures everywhere. Most people know that ancient civilizations were slave societies. But few know where all these slaves came from and what was in their hearts and minds. The mythological concept of the Abyss or the Void ensured that the origins of the slaves remained obscure and unimportant, at least to believers. When the Goddess cultures of the world are put back into the picture, then the origins of the slaves, the artisans, the farmers, and the women become clear and we can imagine their role as patriarchy established itself.

Over centuries full of turbulence and conflict, human populations moved from the ancestral homelands into villages and cities around the private estates. Conceiving the rise of Greek mythology as part of this movement gives some historical grounding to understand its role in human culture. The pantheon of the gods of Mount Olympus replaced humanity's Goddess predecessors to provide cohesion to the new private property world. Bringing new versions of female goddesses onto Mount Olympus created continuity with the past as the Goddesses of the prehistoric world were re-defined and re-imagined to fit the new world.

27: The Goddess Refused to Die

The first problem Zeus had as supreme commander was snuffing out the remnants of the Goddess still hanging around. The Goddess sneaked into Mount Olympus in the guise of Demeter, Zeus' troublesome sister, and daughter of Rhea. Demeter was the goddess of the harvest and occupied a minor place among all the other majestic gods on Olympus. She had a daughter, Persephone, who was born without a father. Threatened by Demeter's power over the harvest, Zeus conspired with his brother, Hades, to kidnap and rape Persephone.

Demeter and Persephone

Demeter's presence on Mount Olympus is the clearest admission that the Goddess of prehistory was fundamental to the new patriarchal myths. As the Goddess of the harvest, she was the Creator, very similar to the Goddess worshipped in the old world, but now reduced to her function in providing the harvest to the gods.

The harvest was central in the rise of patriarchy. It motivated the seizure of the land. It was the source of wealth that men were pursuing. And here she was giving birth to a daughter to inherit her powers without a father. Just as Ouranos emerged from Gaia without a father, setting up the struggle for supremacy over the earth, so Demeter, Zeus' sister, appeared on Mount Olympus giving birth to a daughter with no father. She threatened Zeus' power and had to be brought under control.

The story of Zeus and Hades' conspiracy to kidnap and rape Persephone mythologizes how patriarchal land owners captured and enslaved women. With no father, Persephone was a woman alone without male protection. This might be a good description of how men stealing the land saw the women of the non-monogamous, matrilineal clans that occupied it.

When Demeter gave birth to Persephone without a father, Persephone was not made into primordial gods as Gaia's immaculately conceived son, Ouranos, was. He became part of the pre-existing stage on which the rest of the drama played out. Not so with Persephone's immaculate conception. Instead, Demeter's fatherless daughter became an unwitting victim of kidnap and rape, and later the queen of the underworld.

In the myth, it all starts one bright sunny day when Persephone is out picking flowers with her lady friends. Persephone was lured to a field full of beautiful flowers, placed there by Zeus so Hades could grab her. She was not alone at the time of the kidnapping.

> *For her daughter was playing with the deep-bosomed maidens of Oceanos and was gathering flowers—roses and crocuses and fair violets in the soft meadow and lilies and hyacinths and the narcissus that the earth brought forth as a snare for the fair-faced maiden by the counsel of Zeus and to please the lord of many guests. Wondrously bloomed the flower, a marvel for all to see, whether deathless gods or mortal men. From its root grew forth a hundred blossoms, and with its fragrant*

odor the wide heaven above and the whole earth laughed, as did the salt wave of the sea. Then the maiden marveled and stretched forth both her hands to seize the fair plaything, but the wide-wayed earth gaped ... and up rushed the prince, the host of many guests, the many-named son of Cronos, with his immortal horses. Against her will he seized her and drove her off weeping in his golden chariot, but she screamed aloud, calling on Father Cronides, the highest of gods and the best.

But no immortal god or mortal man heard her voice (in fact, not even the rich-fruited olive trees heard her), none except the daughter of Persaios, Hecate of the fair veil, as she was thinking delicate thoughts. She, along with Prince Helios, the glorious son of Hyperion, heard the cry from her cave, heard the maiden calling on Father Cronides. But he sat far off apart from the gods in his prayer-filled temple, receiving fine victims from mortal men....[46]

Kidnapping Persephone to make her the queen of the underworld put women in their place in Zeus's world. Certainly Hades needed a Queen given that women would have been the first to resist the male usurpation and thus fall into the underworld. So establishing the woman's place in Hades was essential to the future of the male gods.

Demeter's story evoked a vision of the historical roots of the transition to patriarchy. The flowers that lure Persephone to the place where Hades could grab her symbolize the crops, the herbs, the knowledge of medicinal plants that women of the ancient world had created. As she reached for the flowers, the earth opened up and Hades grabbed her. The Devil rises up from the ground to grab the maiden, an act revealing the transformation of the land itself from sacred source of life to the home of the devil. Male usurpation of the land gave the devil the pathway to kidnap women. He drives off with her in his golden chariot, symbolizing the limitless wealth from the earth now possessed by male property owners. Zeus and Hades worked well together in the betrayal of their sister.

That no one heard the cries of the abducted Persephone is another image of the early phases of the war against women. The people of the ancient Goddess world were too busy with their "delicate thoughts" in their prayer filled temples. The beginnings of the male usurpation of the land might have gone down peacefully at first as the ancient world remained preoccupied with its own reality.

> *Now, so long as the goddess beheld the earth and the starry heaven and the tide of the teeming sea and the rays of the sun, so long as she still hoped to behold her dear mother and the tribes of the eternal gods, just so long, despite her sorrow, hope warmed her high heart. But then rang the mountain peaks and the depths of the sea to her immortal voice, and her lady mother heard her.*[47]

In the early times of the transition to patriarchy, hope lived on. Demeter finally heard Persephone's call as the ancient world awoke to the meaning of the abduction and the male usurpation of the land.

Then sharp pain caught at her [Demeter's] heart, and with her hands she tore the veil about her ambrosial hair and cast a dark mantle about her shoulders, and then she sped like a bird over land and sea, searching. But there was none who would tell the truth to her; neither god nor mortal man, not even a bird, a soothsaying messenger, came near her. Thereafter for nine days Lady Deo [Demeter] roamed the earth with torches burning in her hands, nor ever in her sorrow did she taste ambrosia and sweet nectar, nor bathe her body. But when at last the tenth morning came to her with the light, Hecate met her, a torch in her hands, and spoke a word of tidings, saying:

"Lady Demeter, you who bring the seasons, you giver of glad gifts, which of the heavenly gods or mortal men has ravished away Persephone and brought sorrow to your heart? For I heard a voice, but I saw not with my eyes who the ravisher was. All this I say to you truly."

Hecate joins the search for someone to tell them who did it. Demeter's search for her daughter is joined by other gods who realize what a great wrong had been committed against the harvest queen. Then they come upon Helios:

So they came to Helios, who watches both gods and men, and stood before his horses, and the lady goddess questioned him:

Helios, have pity on me who am a goddess, if ever by word or deed I gladdened your heart. My daughter, whom I bore, a sweet plant and fair to see—it was her clear voice I heard through the air

> *that bears no crops, like the voice of a woman being forced, but I saw her not with my eyes. But you who look down with your rays from the bright sky upon all the land and sea, tell me truly concerning my dear child, if you did behold her. Who it is that has gone off and ravished her away from me against her will? Who is it of gods or mortal men?*

Helios reveals the terrible truth:

> *There is none other responsible of the immortals but Zeus himself, the gatherer of clouds, who gave your daughter to Hades, his own brother, to be called his lovely wife.*[48]

Demeter is shocked at her brother's betrayal. Here she is a goddess having joined the gods of male supremacy on Mount Olympus only to realize that she was being used, betrayed and stabbed in the back. She did not passively accept Zeus' will and bow in submission. No, she rebelled and abandoned Mount Olympus. She threw down the gauntlet in the face of the new patriarchal gods. Her faith in Zeus could not withstand the brutality of the abduction and rape of her daughter.

Horrified at Zeus' betrayal, Demeter resumed searching for her daughter.

28: Adapting to Patriarchy

Demeter's search takes her into the new world that patriarchy had created. The first thing that happens after Demeter abandons Mount Olympus, disguised as an old woman, is that pirates abduct her and take her by ship to a faraway port to sell her into slavery. Like the slave ships off the coast of Africa in the modern era, pirates grab women for sale to new patriarchal masters.

But Demeter escapes from the pirates. She continues wandering in the far away lands until she comes to a town square where she joins a group of women drawing water from the town well.

> *Who are you, old woman, and of what ancient folk? And why were you wandering apart from the town, not drawing near to the houses where in the shadowy halls there are women of your own age, and younger too, who may treat you kindly in word and deed?* [49]

This is another powerful image of the early settlements that formed around the patriarchal farms and villages. The women quickly take Demeter into their circle and find her a job with a noble family as a nanny for their children.

Demeter was a good nanny. She raised the noble children with love. But as she got close to one child, she tried to make the child immortal, like her. To do this, the story goes, she gets ready to throw the child into the hearth fire. However, the child's eldest sister sees her and summons the family who stop her from doing it. A goddess throwing a child into the fire to obtain immortality dramatizes the vast gulf between the new patriarchal society and the ancient goddess cultures that surrounded them.

Of course, you might say, I would have stopped her from throwing the child into the fire, too. But remember, this is the patriarch's story, told from the point of view of the new sky gods. You might imagine a similar situation with the white child of a slave owner loving the black nanny who had cared for her growing up. What would the slave owners think of the daughter's loyalty and love for her nanny leading to her joining an interracial world? Horror and outrage, beatings and exile for the child would seem preferable to allowing the interracial love to flourish. The slave owning father might well conceive of losing his child to interracial love as tantamount to throwing the child into a fire. The fire is the hell that interracial families experience in the white world.

When the mortal family stops the immortal goddess from granting immortality to one of the family's children, Demeter sees that there is no way back to the goddess culture.

> *O helpless and uncounseled race of men, who know not beforehand the fate of coming good or coming evil. For, behold, you have wrought upon yourself a bane incurable by your own witlessness. For by the oath of the gods, the relentless water of Styx, [river separating the world from the underworld] I would have made your dear child deathless and exempt from age forever and would have given him glory imperishable. But now in no way may he escape*

… death, yet glory imperishable will ever be his, since he has lain on my knees and slept within my arms. But as the years go round, the sons of the Eleusinians will ever wage war and dreadful strife, one upon the other. I am the honored Demeter, the greatest good and gain to the immortals and mortal men. But, come now, let all the people build me a great temple and an altar beside, below the town and the steep wall, above Callichoros on the jutting rock. But I myself will prescribe the rites, so that in time to come you may duly perform them and appease my power.[50]

Her world is rejected, even by the eldest daughter of the family, a daughter who reached maturity without a goddess-like nanny to confuse her. Achieving immortality by throwing the child into the fire is a vision embodying the patriarchal nightmare of returning to the Abyss, a stand-in for the goddess cultures. The role of the eldest daughter in helping to stop Demeter from throwing the child into the fire dramatizes the real divisions among women that arose as women adapted to the new world and adopted the patriarchal gods.

Demeter's horror at the family's action preventing her from making the child immortal causes her to exclaim that mortals "have wrought upon yourself a bane incurable by your own witlessness." By rejecting the goddess, they doomed themselves to mortality, to aging and dying. They also put Demeter in her place in the new patriarchal world controlled by Zeus. This rejection of immortality is a preview of the story of Adam and Eve who tumble out of the

Garden of Eden for similar witlessness when they get caught eating the fruit from the forbidden tree of knowledge of good and evil.

Demeter's demand for a great temple and an altar in the town echoes Black Elk's sacred woman's tepee in the center of the village. But the differences are stark. In Black Elk's story, the sacred woman's tepee was a pillar of the whole culture. In Demeter's case, her temple was a rebel stronghold, a temporary refuge from the powers of the slave masters.

Rejected, Demeter turns her back on the mortals and stops the harvests by withholding her powers, bringing humankind into a severe crisis. The early war against women must have unsettled the ancient world for centuries while generations passed and people adapted to the new powers of private property.

Demeter's rebellion, holed up in her separate temple, was not acceptable to Mount Olympus. Zeus needed the harvests. He could not kill Demeter as he did his other enemies in his wars. He had to find a way to control her. He could not allow the ancient supremacy of the goddess world to live on independently inside his town.

> *Now the whole race of mortal men would have perished utterly from the stress of famine, and the gods who hold mansions in Olympos would have lost the share and renown of gift and sacrifice, if Zeus had not taken note and conceived a counsel within his heart.*[51]

Zeus had Hades kidnap Persephone with the hope she would go quietly to hell. But Demeter stopped the harvest until her daughter was freed. Now Zeus had to persuade Demeter to be reasonable. What is in a kidnapper's heart, even if he is a god? Asserting his power, through force or trickery seems to be it. So Hades played a trick on Persephone. Hades enticed or forced (depending on who is telling the story) Persephone to eat the pomegranate seed. It is the ancient predecessor of biting the apple in the garden of Eden, with Hades playing the role of the snake. It compromised Persephone, who was unaware of the implications of eating food taken from the devil himself.

Zeus persuades Hades "to bring up holy Persephone from the murky gloom into the light and among the gods, so that her mother might behold her and relent from her anger." As Persephone rose to join her mother, Hades "gave her a sweet pomegranate seed to eat, and this he did so that she might not abide forever beside revered Demeter...." When she rejoins Demeter, the first thing her mother said was "Child, have you eaten any food in Hades?" She might also have asked if she enjoyed her ride in the golden chariot. Or did she like being the queen of the underworld.

> *For if you have not [eaten anything], then with me and your father, the son of Cronus, who has dark clouds for his dwelling, shall you ever dwell honored among all the immortals. But if you have tasted food, you must return again and beneath the hollows of the earth dwell in Hades a third portion of the year. Yet two parts of the year you shall abide with me and the other immortals. When the earth blossoms with all manner of fragrant spring flowers, then from beneath the murky gloom*

> *shall you come again, a mighty marvel to gods and to mortal men.*[52]

Persephone confesses to her mother that "Hades himself stealthily compelled me to taste a sweet pomegranate seed against my will." Eating the pomegranate seed wedded Persephone to the devil's world. It dramatizes the shift from the ancient balanced diet to the grain based diet of the new farms of patriarchy. Controlling the food resources of colonized people has always given the suppliers great power.

Persephone had eaten from the Devil's hand which meant that from then on the goddess of the harvest had to share her knowledge with the devil. Persephone's dark fate foretold the future of the women who produced 80% of the sustenance for the people. She had unleashed the magical richness of the harvest, and now had to give it over to the patriarchal rulers. Zeus and Hades now had the harvest queen where they wanted her.

If I put this transition into the more earthly framework of the historical transition from the Goddess to patriarchy, it might look like a simple deed for an kidnapping extortionist. He owned the land. She had to eat. It was a natural solution to his problem. Starve them into submission. It was as simple as one-two-three. Take their land, capture them, and starve them into submission. The pomegranate seed symbolized the transition.

Meanwhile, back in Zeus' town, a problem remained as long as Demeter was holed up in her new independent temple. Zeus had Demeter cornered.

Without her daughter, now abducted by the Devil, she faced a bleak existence even in her separate temple down below the town. Women still did all the agriculture, weaving, domestication of animals, and so much more. So as long as Demeter withheld her knowledge, a threat to production and a disruption of 'normality' remained. It was no small matter.

Zeus' sends Demeter's mother, Rhea, to talk some sense into her.

> *But to them as a messenger did far-seeing Zeus of the loud thunder send fair-haired Rhea to bring dark-mantled Demeter among the gods, with pledge of what honor she might choose among the immortals. He vowed that her daughter for the third part of the revolving year should dwell beneath the murky gloom, but for the other two parts she should abide with her mother and the other gods.*[53]

When Demeter hesitated and the spring failed to bring forth the new harvests, Rhea pleaded with Demeter to return to Mount Olympus and assume her place among the immortal gods. Rhea spoke to Demeter:

> *Come here, child; for he calls you, far-seeing Zeus, the loud thunderer, to come among the gods, and has promised you such honors as you desire and has decreed that your child for a third of the rolling year shall dwell beneath the murky gloom, but the other two parts with her mother and the rest of the immortals. He promises that it shall be so and nods his head in agreement. But come, my child,*

> *obey, and be not too unrelenting against the son of Cronos, the lord of the dark cloud. And quickly make grow the grain that brings life to men.*[54]

Rhea prevails over Demeter and the deal is made. Demeter meekly returns to Mount Olympus accepting her daughter's continued captivity, one third of the time anyway.

> *Demeter of the fair garland obeyed. Speedily she sent up the grain from the rich soil, and the wide earth was heavy with leaves and flowers. She hastened and showed the care of her rites to the verdict-pronouncing kings.... Now when the goddess had given instruction in all her rites, they went to Olympos, to the gathering of the other gods. There the goddesses dwell beside Zeus who delights in the thunderbolt; holy and revered are they.*[55]

Demeter returns to her role as a minor goddess in Mount Olympus and gives up all her ancient knowledge to the Olympic male gods. The sky gods triumphed over the earth gods as women took their place at the knee of Zeus. Demeter's return to Mount Olympus was more than giving up her ancient knowledge and restoring the harvest. She also gave up her body when she moved from her temple to Mount Olympus. In doing so, she accepted the powers of the sky gods, a spiritual transformation of profound importance. Future generations of women were doomed to follow Persephone's fate as part time queens of the underworld. It was a compromise that could not last.

29: Patriarchy's Big Problem: Displaced Humanity

When patriarchal conquest occurred, people who survived were forced out of their known world. Their cultures were destroyed and their relatives scattered to the winds. They became displaced humanity: workers, slaves, artisans, and servants wandering the streets looking for work. The new owners and their gods had to figure out how to deal with them.

> *You know, the gods never have let on*
> *How humans might make a living. Else,*
> *You might get enough done in one day*
> *to keep you fixed for a year without working.*
> *You might just hang your plowshare up in the smoke,*
> *And all the fieldwork done by your oxen*
> *And hard-working mules would soon run to ruin.*[56]

Humans "making a living" was a new way of life, fundamentally different from the cultures of the Goddess. Making a living through slavery, wage labor, or independent contracting on privately owned farms had little to do with harmonizing life in the natural world. It was now a matter of exploiting nature, of extracting wealth under orders from and for the benefit of the owner.

The new land owners knew very well what it was like to "get enough done in one day to keep you fixed for a year without working" as that was the epitome of the life of nobility. If everyone aspired to such idleness, you would certainly "run to ruin." Who's ruin? The land owners' ruin. Even the gods had to get their cut of the harvest. People could be perfectly happy kicking back for the year. The land would be happy to take a breather from the plow. What is the problem? Income to the land owners stops, is the problem. Zeus had to find a way to keep displaced people working.

The Woman's Place

Women were central to solving this problem. Changing how people survived also impacted the family because the status of women in this transition from prehistory to civilization included more than their role as workers. It created the problem of the human family outside the fence line which was fundamental to the status of women and the family.

In the prehistoric world, the family evolved around a circle of women supported and protected by the whole clan, including the men. As Sjöö and Mor put it:

> *"Among humans, males help with protection and food acquisition; but it is the communal group of females that surrounds the child, in its first four to six years of life, with a strong physical, emotional, traditional, and linguistic presence. And this is the foundation of social life and human culture."*[57]

What happened to this core social foundation of human culture in the transition to private property? It was suppressed as "promiscuous" behavior of "savages" and replaced by the monogamous family on a private estate, or under a bridge or in a hut somewhere depending on your status and wealth. The wider clan support for women and children disappeared along with the cultures of the conquered tribes. Along the way, new settler gods worked their way into the social fabric of the displaced masses creating a range of adaptations. The more that the lower levels of society conformed to the settler monogamous ideals and religions, the further the status of women sank.

How did sexual relations move from the mother's clan to the displaced world of workers and slaves growing up around private property? Both men and women left their homelands to join the new world. Sexual and family relations traveled with them. Among land owners, monogamy was the name of the game. Among the displaced, monogamy was the ideal of the new rulers, a far off ideal that people might aspire to.

When men and women hooked up outside the confines of their indigenous cultures, they had to find new ways of building relationships and families. The immediate reality of the newly displaced people was one of slavery, scarcity, hunger, and strife which would have tended to break up relationships and subject people to hardships unknown before. People, men and women, might leave their homelands with no idea of what awaited them. Stories might have filtered back to the tribes about it, but stories alone would not prepare people for the impact of what awaited them. The shock left by such a traumatic change would have left sexual relationships for men and women in limbo. Descriptions of the American slave system have made this abundantly clear.

In the context of the displaced masses experiencing the male led drive to capture and subordinate women, it is easy to imagine the rise of prostitution and brothels everywhere. They would arise in response to the sexual urges of the displaced, not to mention the wanderlust of monogamous men stepping out on their wives. Women would find a way to survive and men would find a way to have sex.

Just as men imposed monogamy upon women in order to secure their claims on the land, men also imposed slavery upon their work forces to ensure their possession of the harvest. Prostitution and "promiscuity" must have arisen for the great masses of the population surrounding the new class of property owners from the very start. The wars to conquer the land were the same as the wars to conquer women. Along with war, monogamy and slavery were both fundamental expressions of the new system of private property. The mythological expression of this transition could not be more blatant. Demeter's and Persephone's acceptance of their status as part time minor gods had grave consequences.

30: Hiding Fire

Zeus needed an incentive to get people to work. The warrior king used deprivation to have his way. Punishment was big in patriarchy from the start. So Zeus decided to make life hard for humans by hiding fire. But it did not work out as planned as fire did not stay hidden for long.

> *He [Zeus] hid fire. But that fine son of Iapetos stole it*
> *Right back out from under Zeus' nose, hiding*
> *The flame in a fennel stalk. And thundering Zeus*
> *Who rides herd on the clouds got angry and said:*
> *"Iapetos' [God of Mortality] boy, if you're not the*
> *   smartest of them all!*
> *I bet you're glad you stole fire and outfoxed me.*
> *But things will go hard for you and for humans after*
> *   this.*
> *I'm going to give them Evil in exchange for fire,*
> *Their very own Evil to love and embrace."*[58]

Fire, a stand-in for technology, could not stay hidden because it arose from the work and genius of the common people, including women, not from the idle land owners who wanted to steal it along with the land. Once defeated in his attempt to hide it, Zeus, laughing, allowed humans to keep fire and along with it gave them their very own Evil "to love and embrace."

How did giving humanity 'Evil' compensate Zeus for the loss of the secret of fire? Certainly evil must have existed within the Goddess world before patriarchy. The captives and displaced wanderers undoubtedly carried it with them into town along with their fig leaves. It never rose, however, to the importance that it now assumed within the new patriarchal world.

The difference is that displaced humanity could now call on evil in their struggles for advantage and survival. In the cultures of the Goddess, evil lacked such a social role in the context of the communal values of the tribe which provided for everyone. Everybody in. Nobody out. The owners had their own separate evil used in their usurpation of the land, and from their capturing and enslaving of women and workers. The myth makers see the workings of this evil very clearly among the immortals, and decide to give mortals "their very own Evil to love and embrace." A society divided by property ownership emerged with a double standard when it came to Evil.

The secret of fire is the knowledge of the way to survive, or in modern terminology, the means of production. As Demeter's story shows, owners of the land needed the displaced people's knowledge to make a go of it. So Zeus, the owners' god, never really had fire to keep as a secret. His secret was the use of fire in creating the wealth for the owners of the stolen land. If humans realized that their work and their knowledge were the enabling factors in the power of the land owners, it would threaten the owner's hold on power. Giving humanity their very own Evil compensated for Zeus' loss of fire by dividing and weakening humanity. It offered ambitious slaves and serfs a way up the ladder of success by embracing evil. Evil became an institutional avenue for upward mobility within the displaced world. Divide and rule became the *modus operandi* of the new ruling groups.

Viewed in historical terms, it is known that the Goddess-centered world had created the basic tools of agriculture before patriarchy ever existed. That included fire, domestication of plants and animals, and the tools of the artisan trades including weaving, mining and smelting of metals. The historic moment when the Greek myths appeared coincides with the end of the Bronze Age (3300 to 1200 BC) and the beginning of the Iron Age. The essence of the Bronze age is the state monopoly of bronze metal technology and its use in armed warfare and agriculture. Keeping bronze technology a secret was a top state priority. When the Iron Age dawned, the ancient empires faced the results of the secrets getting out. It was technology that the commoner could and did master. Commoners could make iron tools and weapons in their backyards. It contributed to the undoing of the ancient world. Put into this historical (archaeological) framework, the ancient myths seem to arise like sublimated dreams of the despotic patriarchs.

Zeus sent a woman to sow these seeds of Evil among the people. A woman created by the gods, not by the procreative powers of females. A woman named Pandora.

31: **Pandora**

Zeus did not send an immortal to pass out evil. Not Demeter born of Rhea, or Persephone born of Demeter. No one born from a woman, it seems, immortal or mortal could do the job. Instead, Zeus had the ugliest god among the beautiful immortals, the god of fire, Hephaistos, create Pandora out of clay with her box full of troublesome qualities.

> *Then he called Hephaistos*
> *And told him to hurry and knead some earth and water*
> *And put a human voice in it, and some strength,*
> *And to make the face like an immortal goddess' face*
> *And the figure like a beautiful, desirable virgin's.*
> *Then he told Athena to teach her embroidery and*
>   *weaving,*
> *And Aphrodite golden to spill grace on her head*
> *And painful desire and knee-weakening anguish.*
> *And he ordered the quicksilver messenger, Hermes,*
> *To give her a bitchy mind and a cheating heart.*
> *That's what he told them, and they listened to Lord*
>   *Zeus,*
> *Cronos' son. And right away famous old Gimpy*
> *Plastered up some clay to look like a shy virgin*
> *Just like Zeus wanted, and the owl-eyed goddess*
> *Got her all dressed up, and the Graces divine*
> *And Lady Persuasion put some gold necklaces*
> *On her skin, and the Seasons (with their long, fine hair)*
> *Put on her head a crown of springtime flowers.*
> *Pallas Athena put on the finishing touches,*
> *And the quicksilver messenger put in her breast*
> *Lies and wheedling words and a cheating heart,*
> *Just like rumbling Zeus wanted. And the gods' own*
>   *herald*
> *Put a voice in her, and he named that woman*

*Pandora, because all the Olympians donated
    something,
And she was a real pain for human beings.*[59]

Zeus gave Pandora and her box of troubles to
Epimetheus, the brother of Prometheus, the two of
whom acted as representatives of mankind among
the gods. Prometheus warned against accepting gifts
from Zeus but to no avail.

*When this piece of irresistible bait was finished,
Zeus sent Hermes to take her to Epimetheus
As a present, and the speedy messenger-god did it.
Epimetheus didn't think on what Prometheus had told
    him,
Not to accept presents from Olympian Zeus but to send
    any
Right back, in case trouble should come of it to mortals.
No,
Epimetheus took it, and after he had the trouble
Then he thought on it.
Because before that the human race
Had lived off the land without any trouble, no hard
    work,
No sickness or pain that the Fates give to men
(And when men are in misery they show their age
    quickly).
But the woman took the lid off the big jar with her hands
And scattered all the miseries that spell sorrow for men.
Only Hope was left there in the unbreakable container,
Stuck under the lip of the jar, and couldn't fly out.
The woman clamped the lid back on the jar first,
All by the plan of the Aegisholder, cloud-herding Zeus.
But ten thousand or so other horrors spread out among
    men,
The earth is full of evil things, and so's the sea.
Diseases wander around just as they please, by day
    and by night,*

> *Soundlessly, since Zeus in his wisdom deprived them of voice.*
> *There's just no way you can get around the mind of Zeus.*[60]

The myth has Evil coming to men through a woman made of clay. In light of the ubiquity of clay statues of the female Goddess during prehistoric times, this usurpation of the clay figure of a woman to serve Zeus as the sower of trouble and strife clearly reflects its purpose to use the powerful symbols of the ancient world. It draws on the deep awareness of the female Goddess figures that must have existed everywhere among prehistoric humanity. Now this ubiquitous clay figure was turned to a new purpose. Named Pandora, she acted much like the snake in Biblical times. The snake and women transformed from familiar revered old symbols of renewal into purveyors of evil.

It was another step in the decline and fall of the Goddess among displaced people. Her central role in prehistory, forgotten and denied, was now replaced by a clay illusion who sowed strife and discord while maintaining hope for something better. Coming out of the ancient Goddess world, mortals who succumbed to Pandora lost their beloved spiritual leader as they wandered the land looking for riches in a competitive nightmare of imposed scarcity.

Zeus' failure to hide fire from mortals left open the possibility that "the human race ... [could continue to live] off the land without any trouble, no hard work. No sickness or pain that the Fates give to men." As much as Edith Hamilton might have liked to believe otherwise, the assumptions underlying Zeus' clay woman reveals that the prehistoric world was not so bad. Humanity could and did live off the land without any trouble with a balanced diet and healthy lifestyle for thousands of years. How else could humanity's numbers have grown into the millions in every corner of the Earth before civilization? Settler land thefts pushed traditional ancient cultures into the margins when it did not just obliterate them. The displaced prehistoric populations were refugees from destroyed cultures that had lasted thousands of years without damaging the earth and without war or slavery. In other words, easy marks for armed conquest.

No longer in the matrilineal clans, united by ancient cultures, the wanderers now confronted each other as competitors for resources made scarce by private property. The new scarcity replaced prehistoric sharing within a cooperative world. So Pandora is injected into the souls of displaced humanity with her jar full of troubles. The old female Goddess figures just did not fit the realities of the civilized world.

In the modern age, it is hard to imagine the depth and meaning of the spiritual content of the prehistoric cultures. Some inkling of its depths becomes apparent as we try to understand how these ancient prehistoric cultures created astronomically precise monuments such as Stonehenge, Chaco Canyon, Machu Picchu in Peru, and many others all over the world. The shamans of the old world passed on their secrets in the oral traditions of these cultures. In the patriarchal transformation, individuals were forced to flee their native lands, to abandon their contacts with the families and clans who gave birth to them, to forget ancestors stretching back over the tens of thousands of years of prehistory and to stop speaking their languages. Such strong cultural ties to the Goddess world would not die easily. It had to happen over generations. This is the milieu in which the new religions took root. Greek gods on Mount Olympus offered displaced wanderers new leaders to help them adapt to the world outside the warm embrace of ancient sharing and peace that private property destroyed.

32: The Five Ages of the Greek Gods Ended Badly

Greek mythology's imperfect gods and compromises ultimately brought an end to their heavenly reign. Ancient writer Apollodorus outlined the five ages of Greek mythology that chronicled this process of decline. The five Greek ages of his poem idealized the emergence and decline of the ancient empires and their gods. Putting the Goddess into the narrative yields interesting insights into the prehistoric processes of the transition to patriarchy.

1. The Golden Age

Golden was the first race of articulate folk
Created by the immortals who live on Olympos.
They actually lived when Cronus was king of the sky,
And they lived like gods, not a care in their hearts,
Nothing to do with hard work or grief,
And miserable old age didn't exist for them.
From fingers to toes they never grew old,
And the good times rolled. And when they died
It was like sleep just raveled them up.
They had everything good.
The land bore them fruit
All on its own, and plenty of it too. Cheerful folk,
They did their work peaceably and in prosperity,
With plenty of flocks, and they were dear to the gods.
And sure when Earth covered over that generation,
They turned into holy spirits, powers above ground,
Invisible wardens for the whole human race.
They roam all over the land, shrouded in mist,
Tending to justice, repaying criminal acts
And dispensing wealth. This is their royal honor. [61]

The myth of the Golden Age suggests the nature of the world at the time when the first male land thieves set upon the commons to claim them for themselves alone. These were the pioneers of land theft, the pilgrims of civilization, who went about their usurpation in innocence and ignorance. Generous and tolerant Goddess cultures might have observed them without fear, tolerating them without seeing the ultimate threat that they posed for the future. "A new breed of men sent down from heaven" said Virgil some centuries later. No hard work, no old age, plenty and abundance everywhere. And when these first thieves died, they became holy spirits, "invisible wardens for the whole human race." Examples for all men to emulate, enshrined in mythology for all to worship.

When men first took possession of land, they might have lived in harmony with the Goddess cultures for some time. These new landowners were the ones who first conceived of male gods to give holy sanction to their acts of usurpation. The idealized memory of this Golden Age had the gods creating the first land owners in a time before the conflicts arose and conquests of Goddess cultures succeeded.

> *The Golden Age was first; when Man, yet new,*
> *No rule but uncorrupted Reason knew:*
> *And, with a native bent, did good pursue.*
> *Unforc'd by punishment, un-aw'd by fear.*
> *His words were simple, and his soul sincere;*
> *Needless was written law, where none opprest:*
> *The law of Man was written in his breast.*[62]

These first land grabbers were surrounded by a peaceful way of life that had lasted for millennia. In a description fitting the modern food forests of permaculture, the myth waxes on: "The land bore them fruit / All on its own, and plenty of it too." At first, everyone might have benefited from it. The Golden Age honeymoon evokes visions similar to the new world myth of the hardy pilgrims landing on the shores of North America being greeted by turkey-toting Indians, happily sharing the bounty of the earth. But the honeymoon did not last, even in the myths. The first generation which did not age, nevertheless passed on.

2. The Silver Age

Then the Olympians made a second generation they called the Silver Age, "not nearly so fine as the first..." The Olympians, not women, gave birth to these first two generations. The myth makers couldn't help themselves. They just had to remove the woman's role in creating humanity and place it instead in the hands of their male gods.

> *Later, the Olympians made a second generation,*
> *Silver this time, not nearly so fine as the first,*
> *Not at all like the gold in either body or mind.*
> *A child would be reared at his mother's side*
> *A hundred years, just a big baby, playing at home.*
> *And when they finally did grow up and come of age,*
> *They didn't live very long, and in pain at that,*
> *Because of their lack of wits. They just could not*
>   *stop*
> *Hurting each other and could not bring themselves*
> *To serve the Immortals, nor sacrifice at their altars*
> *The way men ought to, wherever and whenever.*

> *So Zeus, Cronos' son, got angry and did away with them*
> *Because they weren't giving the Blessed Gods their honors.*[63]

The silver generation, then, lived at a time when the conflicts between the patriarchal land grabbers and the goddess centered people living all around them first arose in earnest. The first and second generations of gods correspond to the era of Ouranos and Cronus, both of whom did not trust their children. Ouranos cast them into the Earth, aka, Gaia's womb. Cronus swallowed them, keeping them in the male world. Zeus arose in the third generation to make war on Cronus to assume absolute power. So this Silver Age describes the time when patriarchy inched along trying to find a firm footing in the surrounding Goddess-centered world and realized it was going to be war.

Apollodorus did not care for this silver generation very much. The children reared at the newly captured mother's side stayed home too long becoming big babies unfit for the new commercial farm work that the owners demanded. After they reached adulthood, the children quickly died. They quarreled and injured each other.

A woman might have taken her children back to her mother's clan, much to the chagrin of the man stuck on his plot of land. In the epoch of the war to destroy the matrilineal clans, the males who were reared in the Goddess worshiping clans and remained with the clans probably became the subject of derision and hatred. And they probably did not live long in captivity.

Worst of all, Silver Age workers and slaves could not bring themselves to serve the immortals but instead fought all the time with each other, just as Pandora had planned. How disappointing to the slave owners to witness slave rebellions and malcontents among their workers!

The people of the Silver Age, Apollodorus lamented, did not worship the Olympic gods nearly enough. Fully formed by the Goddess cultures, these people entered the patriarchal world unfit and untrustworthy. They did not last long, very much like the experience of the California tribes when they were captured and forced into the Catholic Missions to serve God. It took another generation or two of mortals, growing up outside the goddess cultures, to make the transition to worship the new gods. Such a view of the silver generation fits well with the modern experience of indigenous people forced to assimilate into civilization. It was an age of untrustworthy children.

3. The Bronze Age.

So along came the third age, the Bronze Age.

> *And when Earth had covered over that generation—*
> *Blessed underground mortals is what they are called,*
> *Second in status, but still they have their honor—*
> *Father Zeus created a third generation*
> *Of articulate folk, Bronze this time, not like*
> *The silver at all, made them out of ash trees,*
> *Kind of monstrous and heavy, and all they cared about*
> *Was fighting and war. They didn't eat any food at all.*
> *They had this kind of hard, untamable spirit.*

> *Shapeless hulks. Terrifically strong. Grapplehook*
>   *hands*
> *Grew out of their shoulders on thick stumps of arms,*
> *And they had bronze weapons, bronze houses,*
> *And their tools were bronze. No black iron back then.*
> *Finally they killed each other off with their own hands*
> *And went down into the bone-chilling halls of Hades*
> *And left no names behind. Astounding as they were,*
> *Black Death took them anyway, and they left the sun's*
>   *light.*[64]

The Bronze Age of the Greek myths evokes the Bronze Age of historical times when the first civilizations arose with armies supplied with bronze weapons. This mythical generation came up out of the war zones around the new civilizations. They joined the wars against the goddess clans and gained honor within patriarchal mythology. They also fought each other for supremacy, for land, for trade routes, for slaves.

These metal weapon wielding warriors consolidated civilizations' hold on the surrounding areas. Cities arose surrounded by outlying tribal enclaves which were transformed into patriarchal satellite supply centers. Urban civilization, never self-sufficient, needed every kind of product from water to food to minerals and slaves. As the actual conquest of the Goddess tribes receded into the past, civilization's warriors turned to conquest of rivals and the capturing of resources like land and water. The mythical description of these early warriors as "monstrous and heavy" people who only "cared about ... fighting and war" gives us an image of the first civilized armies marauding the lands and resources of the matrilineal clans. Leaving death and destruction everywhere they went, these mercenaries died in their own wars for the spoils of their victories. Called "Blessed Mortals" they played their role in the advance of patriarchal civilization and were quickly forgotten, like the slaves who built the pyramids. Next came the Heroic Age.

4. The Heroic Age

So Earth buried that generation too,
And Zeus fashioned a fourth race
To live off the land, juster and nobler,
The divine race of Heroes, also called
Demigods, the race before the present one.
They all died fighting in the great wars,..
And when Death's veil had covered them over,
Zeus granted them a life apart from other men,
Settling them at the ends of the Earth.
And there they live, free from all care,
In the Isles of the Blest, by Ocean's deep stream,
Blessed heroes for whom the life-giving Earth
Bears sweet fruit ripening three times a year. [65]

The Heroic Age takes up the battle for supremacy by big armies of men inside the patriarchal world. Continuous war became the hallmark of civilization. The Heroic Age was for winners. No longer a war against the matriarchal clans, now decimated in the dim past, it was a battle for supremacy and hegemony among men. Its participants became the models for men to follow and were given a plush birth in the after life. They lived off the land (farmers) and became Demigods, Lords of the Manner, embodying the ideal life that ended in a glorious death in great wars. If the nobility of the ancient world could have frozen time, this would have been the time for them. It was a time of warlords fighting glorious battles for supremacy. It evokes the ideals that shaped the brief period of the Middle Ages, or Dark Age, in Europe before the urban rich cut the ground out from under the landed gentry. The ancient world played out these same stages in the growth of civilizations. The forces of technological development pushed relentlessly forward giving rise to the next age, the Iron Age. The age of the warlords ended in disillusionment.

5. The Iron Age

The fifth age, called the Iron Age, followed with bitter disappointment.

> *Then the fifth generation: Broad-browed Zeus*
> *Made still another race of articulate folk*
> *To people the plentiful Earth.*
> *I wish*
> *I had nothing to do with this fifth generation,*
> *Wish I had died before or been born after,*
> *Because this is the Iron Age.*
> *Not a day goes by*
> *A man doesn't have some kind of trouble.*
> *Nights too, just wearing him down. I mean*
> *The gods send us terrible pain and vexation.*
> *Still, there'll be some good mixed in with the evil,*
> *And then Zeus will destroy this generation too,*
> *Soon as they start being born gray around the temples.*
> *Then fathers won't get along with their kids anymore,*
> *Nor guests with hosts, nor partner with partner,*
> *And brothers won't be friends, the way they used to*
>   *be.*
> *Nobody'll honor their parents when they get old*
> *But they'll curse them and give them a hard time,*

> *Godless rascals, and never think about paying them*
> >   *back*
> *For all the trouble it was to raise them.*
> *They'll start taking justice into their own hands,*
> *Sacking each other's cities, no respect at all*
> *For the man who keeps his oaths, the good man,*
> *The just man. No, they'll keep all their praise*
> *For the wrongdoer, the man who is violence incarnate,*
> *And shame and justice will lie in their hands.*
> *Some good-for-nothing will hurt a decent man,*
> *Slander him, and swear an oath on top of it.*
> *Envy will be everybody's constant companion,*
> *With her foul mouth and hateful face, relishing evil.*
> *And then*
> *up to Olympos from the wide-pathed Earth,*
> *lovely apparitions wrapped in white veils,*
> *off to join the Immortals, abandoning humans*
> *There go Shame and Nemesis. And horrible suffering*
> *Will be left for mortal men, and no defense against*
> >   *evil.*[66]

The triumph of patriarchy was solidified by the spread of iron technology in the hands of men. The advance of fire technology allowed any commoner to smelt and shape iron tools and weapons in their backyards. A new age dawned that moved beyond ancient Rome and Greece. The Bronze Age mythology of noble ideals drowned in the spread of the commoner's iron sword, now creating armed competition for everything. The age of iron became the age of unbridled greed and war in competition for the land.

The lament of Apollodorus evokes the impact of 'barbarian' invasions on ancient declining empires. 'Barbarian' invaders arose from patriarchal supply centers surrounding the centers of new civilizations.

Their wars did not weaken patriarchy nor stop the advance of technology. Empires collapsed as elite groups hogged up the spoils of war, commercial farming and trade, submerging the old ruling classes in decadence and greed. A new god was needed. It was a fertile ground for the rise of monotheism.

"I have never been able to conceive of the Creator in human form. That is not our way. The minute we went wrong is when we bought into the conception of the Creator in a human form. We submitted to the male authoritarian church whose sole purpose is to have dominion over The Earth. Because when you have dominion over The Earth, you are not part of The Earth anymore. They mine our minds to get at the essence of our spirit. They poison our minds because we let them. We are disconnected from our spiritual connection to The Earth, we have forgotten that we are part of The Earth. They mine the minerals from the earth and convert them into energy. They mine our minds and our spirit."

-John Trudell.

Part 6: Patriarchy's One God of the Bible

33: Monotheism and Monogamy

The one God myth arose and spread widely from 500 BC continuing for 1000 years until all of Europe and much of the world beyond it became Christian. The rise of Christianity was inseparable from the rapid advance of iron technology in the hands of patriarchal farmers and the proprietors of large and small businesses globally. Iron tools and fire technologies unleashed productivity and created possibilities unknown before in a wide variety of industries from beer making to wagon and boat building, mining and manufacturing of all types.

We don't usually associate rapidly advancing technologies with the end of the ancient empires and the start of the middle ages. But during the epoch of spreading Christianity with its solemn cathedrals and monastic clergy, economic productivity, trade and wealth continued to advance everywhere leading up to the industrial revolution centuries later. Private male owners drove the advance of technology to enhance their wealth and power. Prehistoric cultures continued to empty out into growing towns and villages.

In this long view, monotheism and monogamy in the ancient world appear to me as the third stage in the evolution of western civilization's mythologies. First, the Goddess prevailed around the globe in what Marija Gimbutas called "The Civilization of the Goddess." This early era was characterized by human populations living in harmony with nature, in peace without war.

Then came patriarchy and private property with their drive to domination and the enslavement of women and workers. The Greek gods replaced the Goddess with Zeus and his buddies on privately owned Mount Olympus with its continuous wars, income inequality, and the displacement of humanity from the land.

Third, patriarchal monotheism and monogamy then replaced the compromises of the Greeks with the uncompromising male God ruling alone in the heavens. As the prehistoric female oriented world shrank, private property expanded along with its gods.

Patriarchal creation myths differ from ancient myths that emerged from our prehistoric past. The ancient origin myths arose and were passed down in oral traditions within a culture. The Biblical creation story was the first one with an instructional handbook. Leonard Schlain in his book *The Alphabet Versus the Goddess* revealed how writing itself emerged in history out of patriarchy. The "first book" of history is the Bible. With oral traditions swept away along with the Goddess cultures, the only way for people to receive the "word of God" was through a written instrument. Just like the accountant's ledger ruled the private estate, so now the Bible arose to rule patriarchy. Writing and words gave direction to the patriarchal sword, and later, the patriarchal gun.

So I ask myself, how has our biblical origin myth propelled us down a disastrous path? Listening to the Goddess in the background, I began to explore the Bible's story of creation in Book 1, Genesis, a story that was written down 500 BCE at the beginning of the iron age.

The Void

The Biblical story starts with the idea that the world was created 6000 years ago out of a void. Adam was made from dust, Eve was fashioned from Adam's rib, and God gave them dominion over the planet and all life on it.

> *In the beginning God created the heavens and the earth. Now the earth was formless and empty, darkness was over the surface of the deep, and the Spirit of God was hovering over the waters.*[67]

A "formless and empty" Earth without gender now replaced the mythical chaos of the Greeks and their gendered primordial gods. The Greek abyss and the Biblical void serve the same purpose of wiping away our Goddess origins in prehistory. From this male God hovering over the waters comes lightness and darkness, the sky (heavens), the dry land, vegetation, trees, morning and evening, and so on. The Biblical writers had wiped the slate clean. In the beginning, nothing existed except its one male God.

Then God said,

> *Let us make mankind in our image, in our likeness, so that they may rule over the fish in the sea and the birds in the sky, over the livestock and all the wild animals, and over all the creatures that move along the ground.*[68]

The Greek gods were, according to Edith Hamilton, made in the image of man. Now, according to the Bible, man was made in the image of God who then granted men dominion over the Earth. God continues:

> *"I give you every seed-bearing plant on the face of the whole earth and every tree that has fruit with seed in it. They will be yours for food. And to all the beasts of the earth and all the birds in the sky and all the creatures that move along the ground—everything that has the breath of life in it—I give every green plant for food." And it was so.*[69]

The void ends with God's creation of everything which he gives to men to do as they please. The Goddess never existed in this story, which not only fails to mention her but also wipes out the entirety of prehistory in the process, shoving it down into the hole of forgetfulness gripping the wandering displaced masses of humanity. Now, Earth and heaven did not give rise to humanity. We did not evolve out of the miracle of life on our planet. We popped up whole from a wave of the magic wand of a male God in the sky, a God who demands loyalty and obedience from all.

This new monotheistic myth fits the needs of the property owners to a tee. Imagine a man staking out a plot of land for himself, tilling the soil with his iron plow, killing all the biota in the ground and creating dust everywhere. The ancient Goddess cultures are nowhere in sight, disappearing along with the balanced landscapes of the natural world, aka wilderness. Now his act of land theft vanishes into the forgotten past as he contemplates the God-given formless "empty" land all around him. This mindset in ancient times is reproduced in the later conquests of the Americas which allowed the conquerors to think of it as empty and to ignore and destroy the millions of inhabitants occupying it. The spiritual oneness of all life of the Goddess cultures became paganism and blasphemy to the conquerors, as prehistoric life was painted out of the picture.

The Bible arose as the handbook of patriarchy out of the patriarchal Jewish culture in the cradle of civilization in the Euphrates and Tigris river valleys. The story came from a struggling nomadic patriarchal people displaced from their homeland, wandering among multiple male ruled cultures claiming ownership of the land and the divine right of kings. These societies, like the Greeks, had their own gods and used them to keep the Jews out. The new biblical mythology arising from the Jewish people in their struggle to find acceptance and a homeland, however, spread like wildfire in the wider world full of displaced people suffering from colonization at the hands of vicious empires.

No wonder that the biblical story of Moses, wandering in the wilderness, appealed to the masses everywhere. The situation of the displaced people around 500 BCE, however, was fundamentally different from the situation of the displaced goddess cultures some eight to ten thousand years earlier. In early prehistoric times, when Goddess cultures prevailed universally, enclaves of private property arose with their male sky gods as exceptions, as little dots in the landscape. Later, as private property enclaves expanded, or conquests from the outside occurred, increasing numbers of people lost contact with their tribes. Generations pass by leaving everyone's tribal origins fading into the dim past. Imagining this sequence within the four ascents of Black Elk's dream, I could see the cultural impact of private property/conquest on people as they went from living within the circle of the people to the time when the circle was broken and people scattered in all directions pursuing their own individual dreams.

Displacement of non-owning Goddess worshiping people was far advanced by the time the Bible appeared. The vitriol and hatred against women centered cultures that permeates the Bible, however, suggests the continuing influence the Goddess still had among the people everywhere.

34: Patriarchy's Second Creation Myth: Adam and Eve

Now no shrub had yet appeared on the earth and no plant had yet sprung up, for the Lord God had not sent rain on the earth and there was no one to work the ground, but streams came up from the earth and watered the whole surface of the ground. Then the Lord God formed a man from the dust of the ground and breathed into his nostrils the breath of life, and the man became a living being.[70]

The new myth has God making man from dust. Not from a woman, not from the creative female force of life visible everywhere. Not from Gaia who had welded society together for thousands of years. Now the Bible asserted that men came into existence without regard to the fact that they were all born from a woman. Greek mythology had done the same thing claiming that Zeus created the five generations. Zeus conjured up Pandora, a woman made out of dust along with her jar of follies. Aphrodite had risen up out of ocean foam bubbling up around the castrated genitals of Ouranos, Zeus' grandfather. All are alternatives to the female womb and are negations of the Goddess.

From the "totality of culture" point of view, it makes sense for the patriarchs to conceptualize the Earth as dry and empty with no shrubs. After all, it comes from the man now confined to his farm, plowing up fields and trading his surplus crops. He removed all the shrubs and trees in the process which is still happening today as industrial agriculture spreads world wide.

Dust resulted from people plowing up the land, leaving it bare. Or from overgrazed pastures reduced to dust by growing herds of domesticated sheep, goats and cattle, no longer free to roam in the wild, no longer subject to predators controlling their numbers. Topsoil blows away in the wind when the age-old root systems are plowed up or destroyed by overgrazing. This is especially true in places like the deserts of the Middle East with its fertile river valleys surrounded by hot deserts. How natural it was to make dust the essential ingredient their God used to create men.

Archaeological, linguistic, and genetic studies tell us that there were vast migrations of Indo-European speakers from the east, people fleeing dry dusty places left from eons of overgrazing and planetary forces of climate change. And later Mongol invasions of pastoral people carried patriarchy along with their armed cavalry and herds of cattle and sheep. Dust, dust everywhere.

> *Now the Lord God had planted a garden in the east, in Eden; and there he put the man he had formed. The Lord God made all kinds of trees grow out of the ground—trees that were pleasing to the eye and good for food. In the middle of the garden were the tree of life and the tree of the knowledge of good and evil. A river watering the garden flowed from Eden... The Lord God took the man and put him in the Garden of Eden to work it and take care of it. And the Lord God commanded the*

man, "You are free to eat from any tree in the garden; but you must not eat from the tree of the knowledge of good and evil, for when you eat from it you will certainly die."[71]

The Garden of Eden embodies our Goddess past when humanity lived in harmony with nature. It is a metaphor for our lost ancestry. Eating from the tree of knowledge and the tree of good and evil was Adam and Eve's great sin. For that, they were expelled. If God put man in the Garden of Eden, and then expelled him, where did he go? Once expelled, humanity was left with the farm, owned by some man with a fence around it, at the mercy of the sky god. The Garden produced plenty of food, but only for those who were allowed to live in it. Once outside it, it was time for "making a living," for work on row crops and life in the slave quarters.

The Lord God said, "It is not good for the man to be alone. I will make a helper suitable for him."

But for Adam no suitable helper was found. So the Lord God caused the man to fall into a deep sleep; and while he was sleeping, he took one of the man's ribs and then closed up the place with flesh. Then the Lord God made a woman from the rib he had taken out of the man, and he brought her to the man. The man said, "This is now bone of my bones and flesh of my flesh; she shall be called 'woman,' for she was taken out of man." That is why a man leaves his father and mother and is united to his wife, and they become one flesh.[72]

Every woman who gives birth to a child knows that she and the child are "one flesh." The origin myth of patriarchy had to find a way to negate this fundamental reality. How else but to make the woman emerge from the man's rib as a subservient being? Then birthing the next generations flowed not from the woman but from the man from whom she was created. She became merely the "vessel" for God's creations. It left the man in charge, free to dominate her along with the planet itself. Talk about a self-serving malicious idea!

35: The Garden of Eden Despiritualized the Earth

As soon as God had fashioned a woman from a man's rib, he put the couple together in the garden where they discovered God monitoring their every move.

Adam and his wife were both naked, and they felt no shame. Now the serpent was more crafty than any of the wild animals the Lord God had made. He said to the woman, "Did God really say, 'You must not eat from any tree in the garden'?" The woman said to the serpent, "We may eat fruit from the trees in the garden, but God did say, 'You must not eat fruit from the tree that is in the middle of the garden, and you must not touch it, or you will die.'" "You will not certainly die," the serpent said to the woman. "For God knows that when you eat from it your eyes will be opened, and you will be like God, knowing good and evil." When the woman saw that the fruit of the tree was good for food and pleasing to the eye, and also desirable for gaining wisdom, she took some and ate it. She also gave some to her husband, who was with her, and he ate it. Then the eyes of both of them were opened, and they realized they were naked; so they sewed fig leaves together and made coverings for themselves. [73]

Without mentioning the Greek myths, the Bible revises its main pillars into the new One God story of Adam and Eve. Here in the Garden of Eden the devil snake tempts them to eat the apple, just as Hades tempted Persephone to eat the pomegranate seed. Hades had tricked Persephone to eat the pomegranate seed to prevent her from returning to Mount Olympus with all the other immortals. Persephone's part-time expulsion from Mount Olympus left women (who did most of the agricultural work) on their own with Hades in charge. The Greeks at least put the Devil in charge of women. Later, the Bible put men in charge of women.

Zeus needed to control mortals (for their own good, of course) and so tried to hide fire from them. Failing to hide fire, Zeus had to find a way to keep mortals "making a living" to prevent them from taking it easy all the time. He fashions Pandora out of clay to sow endless troubles and evil among them, making their lives miserable which would motivate them to keep working. Similarly, the devil-snake exposes God's lie that Adam and Eve will die if they bite the apple. They bite the apple which gets Adam and Eve expelled from the Garden and then punished with endless dusty work and painful childbirth outside the Garden which is now locked up forever.

The Bible traverses the same steps that the Mount Olympus gods took to suppress the Goddess of prehistory. The Greeks put a male god into the world who then fought a long battle to establish his rule over women (the Earth.) The Bible enshrines the demise of the Goddess into a new facade, taking it as a given and then creating a new subservient woman out of Adam's rib. The result is the same. Both the Greeks and the Bible provide theological and spiritual justification for keeping women down.

Unpacking the Story

Adam and Eve find themselves in God's Garden of Eden staring at the forbidden trees of knowledge and good and evil. The serpent comes along and tempts them to eat from the forbidden trees and they do so. Then, having gained wisdom, they feel shame. This simple story's inner meanings became apparent to me in the context of the suppression of the female Goddess.

To begin, who is this serpent? In prehistoric times, snakes held a special place in the world views of all human societies. Marija Gimbutas explains:

> *"Snakes dwell both in water and in the ground. They hibernate in the earth's body during the winter, and they return in spring. Further, their periodic molting reinforced their role as symbols of renewal. Snakes were thus thought to bring life in spring. They were also thought to embody deceased ancestors."* [74]

As a potent symbol of the pre-patriarchal world, snakes become a pariah, a voice from the past calling humans back into unified nature. The snake tempts the woman to eat first, then she tempts the man. The snake, symbol of renewal, goes first to the woman, whose body renews all human life, who then draws the man back into the pre-patriarchal world. Revered and respected ancient symbols, the snake and the woman stand accused of violating God's orders. Just like Iapetos disobeyed Zeus's order to hide fire. Except that now, mortals were not left to their own devices to fight and quarrel among themselves according to the devious plot hatched by Zeus. Now mortals fall under the direct command of God to suffer endless toil and painful childbirth because they did not obey God's word.

The story asserts that eating the fruit from the forbidden tree caused the couple to gain wisdom which leads to shame. What, I asked myself, is the transformation that takes place when they eat the fruit? What is the wisdom gained from eating it? First, remember that this couple consists of the man created from dust and the woman created from his rib. The transformation that takes place is a mental and spiritual one, not a physical one. Both have belly buttons, showing their true origins in the womb of a woman. But both are now in the process of becoming the nuclear family attached to an owned parcel of land, the patriarchal estate.

Adam and Eve glimpse at the old goddess oriented world when they eat the fruit. They then realize that they have betrayed the maternal clan and repudiated the sacredness of the earth. They cannot live in both worlds. Shame is the result of choosing obedience to the male sky god. They are ashamed of their betrayal, not of God's word, but of the ancient customs and beliefs that held human culture together for thousands of years before this betrayal. This fits easily into the actual pre-historical situation. They migrate to the patriarchal estate, walking down from the open forest to the fenced-in land, with fig leaves over their genitals and a need to feel ashamed, standing in open violation of the monogamous ethic of the patriarchs.

Then the man and his wife heard the sound of the Lord God as he was walking in the garden in the cool of the day, and they hid from the Lord God among the trees of the garden. But the Lord God called to the man, "Where are you?" He answered, "I heard you in the garden, and I was afraid because I was naked; so I hid." And he said, "Who told you that you were naked? Have you eaten from the tree that I commanded you not to eat from?"

The man said, "The woman you put here with me—she gave me some fruit from the tree, and I ate it."

Then the Lord God said to the woman, "What is this you have done?"

The woman said, "The serpent deceived me, and I ate."

So the Lord God said to the serpent, "Because you have done this, cursed are you above all livestock and all wild animals! You will crawl on your belly and you will eat dust all the days of your life. And I will put enmity between you and the woman, and between your offspring and hers; he will crush your head, and you will strike his heel." [75]

God curses the snake, the symbol of renewal in the ancient world. This contrasts with Zeus' tolerance of his uncle Iapetos' act of giving fire back to mortals after it was hidden. Zeus did not go to war with Iapetos for his act of theft. Instead he plotted with other gods to create Pandora and sew the seeds of strife, suffering and turmoil among mortals. The new monotheistic God had no problem cursing the snake for this act of disobedience. The snake was chosen because it was the widely respected symbol of renewal and deceased ancestors of the Goddess world. "You will not certainly die," says the snake. And they ate from the tree and did not die.

So the snake was right. They did not die. What happens next reveals much about the nature of this new male god and the impossibility of living in both worlds. Cursing the snake put a curse on the old ways in order to break the hold that ancestors had over their descendants. God's curse on the snake drove a wedge between the couple and the world they were abandoning.

> *To the woman he said, "I will make your pains in childbearing very severe; with painful labor you will give birth to children. Your desire will be for your husband, and he will rule over you."*

In the ancient pre-patriarchal world of matrilineal clans, women and midwives took care of the birthing process. The new vengeful God cursed this network of female independence and solidarity in a way consistent with the new power-oriented male, ignorant and fearful of female self sufficiency. This fear of female self sufficiency arose in the man who chose to break from the old ways and live a new isolated existence clinging to his personal wealth, and his personal piece of the earth. His new God imposed upon this new subservient woman a childbirth full of pain in her new husband's house, away from the circle of women who had always presided over birth and infant care in the ancient circle of the village hearth. Now a husband would rule over her in isolation, even in matters like childbirth that he did not understand and had no business getting into. No business except the business of property inheritance.

> *To Adam he said, "Because you listened to your wife and ate fruit from the tree about which I commanded you, 'You must not eat from it,' cursed is the ground because of you; through painful toil you will eat food from it all the days of your life. It will produce thorns and thistles for you, and you will eat the plants of the field. By the sweat of your brow you will eat your food until you return to the ground, since from it you were taken; for dust you are and to dust you will return."[76]*

When Persephone ate the pomegranate seed she became addicted to the Devil. Zeus and his brother Hades gained control of her through kidnapping, rape and starvation. Now, in the biblical story, man disobeyed God and God put a curse on man, chaining him to labor on the land like a slave. Zeus tried to hide fire. But then, after fire reappeared, Zeus arranged for Pandora's box to give off its Evil temptations in order to divide and rule the displaced masses. Zeus could not afford to let people work one day and be set for the year, leaving the farm to go to ruin (land owners's ruin.)

God's vengeance upon Adam reflects patriarchy's view of dirt and work itself. 'Cursed is the ground' makes it crystal clear. The ground is not sacred, not spiritual, not the source of life, not something to be revered and nurtured in all its complexity and mystery. The ground is now the cursed source of painful toil (work as punishment fit for slaves). Now cursed dirt replaces the balanced world of prehistoric agriculture with forced labor on row crops.

Archaeologists have performed sophisticated chemical analyses on the bones found in early neolithic graves that reveal startling declines in nutrition and health of people living in the new age of patriarchy and private property. Such results contradict the commonly held belief that civilization brought great benefits to the "savages" forced out of their cultures into the bondage of slave oriented civilizations. The curse went on to include eating food from the cursed ground "all the days of your life", enduring thorns and thistles, "for dust you are and to dust you will return". The new slaves of the land were indeed cursed. The new owners in their castles had a good reason to spread the word of this new religion.

> *Adam named his wife Eve, because she would become the mother of all the living.*

To say that the woman made from the dusty man's rib would become the mother of all the living clearly puts the ancestors and cultures that preceded this biblical moment into oblivion.

Yet, the past did not die in spite of God's curses. Zeus could not hide fire and God could not get rid of the Goddess. At this point, I was struck by the strength of the ancient Goddess. Making no mention of Zeus or any of the Greek gods keeps the ancient ambivalence about ancestral female Goddess (Demeter and Persephone) hidden. The male God rules absolutely with no Goddess in heaven anymore. Historically speaking, early patriarchal civilizations arose and declined inside the sea of indigenous people still in the grip of their own goddesses. Women were independent there and lived in ways that the pockets of patriarchal sky god worshiping people sought to destroy.

Non-patriarchal cultures lived on, providing examples and alternatives to the slaves and their descendants, like the African slaves in Florida escaping to the Seminole tribes in the swamps. Losing contact with the oral traditions handed down by matriarchal clans left the new rootless wanderers in a void. The new monotheism had to draw them in.

> *The Lord God made garments of skin for Adam and his wife and clothed them. And the Lord God said, "The man has now become like one of us, knowing good and evil. He must not be allowed to reach out his hand and take also from the tree of life and eat, and live forever." So the Lord God banished him from the Garden of Eden to work the ground from which he had been taken. After he drove the man out, he placed on the east side of the Garden of Eden cherubim and a flaming sword flashing back and forth to guard the way to the tree of life.*[77]

So God drove the man out of the Garden of Eden and locked the gate. Nakedness was over and paradise lost. No more nakedness. The horse could be naked, but not humans. Naked was now evil because it broke the bonds of civilized society, threatening a return to the old ways. The civilized man found the nakedness of the prehistoric world to be promiscuous, the surest way to ruin monogamy and lose his grip on the land. God banished humans from the Garden of Eden precisely because it forever joined them to the Goddess world.

The despiritualization of the Earth that Russell Means lamented flows directly from this mythical expulsion from the Garden of Eden. In prehistory, humans lived in permaculture forests and meadows in harmony with nature. Human cultures came into existence in this setting through the evolutionary processes that gave rise of all life on the planet. Ending this harmonious existence was a product of the rise of private property in the hands of men seeking domination of nature and women for their own profit. This process was what both the Greek myths and the Bible grappled with.

In the Greek myths, Zeus could not afford to leave Demeter in her temple among the city folk. Her powers to stop the harvest meant that she could take down the whole society if her rebellion succeeded. So he compromised with her giving her daughter back to her part time. Demeter returned to Mount Olympus and gave up all her secrets to the male gods, ensuring the male god' supremacy, they hoped.

In the Bible, after Eve and Adam bite the apple, they are expelled forever from the Garden of Eden, and clothed against nakedness. God then cursed Adam with laboring in the fields forever. This was a harsh deal for Adam. It would have been like Zeus making no compromise, but instead, leaving Persephone in hell full time and killing off Demeter. However, if Zeus wanted spring ever to return, (meaning if he wanted women to continue to supply 80% of the food) he could not kill her off. When Demeter gave up all her secrets, the harvest fell into the hands of slave driving land owners. The difference between the Greek myths and the Bible reflects the events on the ground where private property and patriarchy had spread and achieved its full powers.

For women, patriarchy made vast changes in the reproductive life of people. Before, there were no orphans because every child had a mother. In Black Elk's world, they lived in the circle of the people. The child had a father too but the father was not at the center. He was auxiliary, secondary, optional, disposable. Now under patriarchy, sex became the way for a man to create his heirs and to insure the continuation of his line, separate from his mother's line that had prevailed for millennia before.

If all children are guaranteed a place in the maternal clan, there is no reason for monogamy. Virginity becomes unimportant, beyond the thrill of its end enjoyed by both sexes. But once the maternal clan is suppressed, patriarchy required exclusive sexual access and ownership of the woman's body. Banishing Adam and Eve from the Garden of Eden was the symbolic way to banish real men and women from their matrilineal Goddess oriented past. It also destroyed the female circle that gave all children the support of the tribe. The children of poverty, of the unwed, the orphans of the world, are living out the legacy of being expelled from the Garden of Eden set in place thousands of years ago.

36: Prehistory Goes Underground After Conquest

I have to conclude that the change from prehistoric times to historic times is, in essence, the imposition of individual male ownership of the land upon the people of the Earth. This change is at the base of everything. In prehistory, the people lived on the land without owning it. The cultures of prehistoric people were all matrilineal and matrilocal. Not matriarchal. Patriarchal private property meant that instead of the fruits of labor accruing to the mother's clan, they would go to the father and the father's male children. For this to happen, human culture had to transform from collective occupation of the land to a culture where men owned the land as private property. Instead of a culture where women lived independently in woman centered clans and villages, now a woman had to leave her mother's clan, attach herself to a property owner, becoming his property much as the land was his. And she had to adopt his sky gods to replace her earthly Goddess. Men had to keep the woman exclusively to themselves to guarantee that the children were biologically his and that their property would go to their own and not back to the mother's clan. Modern DNA testing is necessary for men wondering about the paternity of a child. With rare exceptions, women need no test to know which child is hers.

Private property and the subjugation of women originate out of the same act of confiscating the land. One could not have happened without the other. And the implications of this transformation were vast. Instead of loving the earth, appreciating its magic, caring for it and sharing it with all the living creatures, the land became God's curse. Earth transformed into dirt and dust, a burden for displaced humanity to bear. The accumulated knowledge of humankind that had been passed down for thousands of years in oral traditions of prehistoric cultures was extorted and transformed into tools to enrich private ownership. Zeus' deal with Demeter and Persephone ended with Demeter giving up all her tricks to the gods of Mount Olympus. Monotheism erased Demeter and her knowledge entirely from the scene.

With the rise of patriarchy, human cultures embarked upon a new journey that required the re-creation of everything. Greek mythology chronicles this transformation. The new ideologies necessarily suppressed women and appropriated their work and knowledge into patriarchy as if women had never done anything before they became male owned.

Women now originated from the rib of a man, not from the female womb. Credit for birthing new generations was expropriated from woman centered, midwife supervised events into a lonely painful process in the dark recesses of male abodes where midwives had to sneak in the back door to help the woman. The role of women in creating language and social life was denied and forgotten in the new creation myths that all began with the day that a man stole a piece of land, an act mythologized as the beginning of the world. The void that preceded these mythical beginnings was blocked out.

Marija Gimbutas focused on the impact of patriarchal blindness on our understanding of prehistory, specifically, in Neolithic Europe.

> *The focus on religion is also significant here. Previous books on Neolithic Europe have focused on habitat, tool kits, pottery, trade, and environmental problems, treating religion as "irrelevant." This is an incomprehensible omission since secular and sacred life in those days were one and indivisible. By ignoring the religious aspects of Neolithic life, we neglect the totality of culture. Archaeologists cannot remain scientific materialists forever, neglecting a multidisciplinary approach. A combination of fields—archaeology, mythology, linguistics, and historical data—provides the possibility for apprehending both the material and spiritual realities of prehistoric cultures. Furthermore, Neolithic social structure and religion were intertwined and were reflections of each other.* [78]

Archaeological remnants do not tell the whole story, but they tell us that prehistoric stories existed and they invite us to wonder about them. Anthropologists call it oral tradition. These stories and ways of life weave together to form culture and language that has wielded us together into a cohesive group that survived and flourished. That is, until they were wiped out or absorbed into settler cultures that conquered them.

It is here, in the act of conquest, that forgetting starts to play its mysterious game, rising like smoke signals through the unchronicled hidden patterns in the lives of the poor and dispossessed everywhere. Call it synergy, mysticism, or whatever, the old ways find life in the transformation of the oppressors' institutions into something unique to a location, a piece of land, a mountain range, an ocean shore where people had lived. At the base of it all is the undeniable fact of birth and female centered early childhood, where women are the source of all our lives and mothers are loved. Patriarchy must reproduce itself every generation through the recreation of misogyny, and the practice of violence against women.

Private Property and the Goddess

Part 7: Conclusion

37: Can We Live in Harmony With Nature?

The prehistoric build-up to the global patriarchal transformation started thousands of years ago. Out of these ancient origins arose a way of life that continues to hold humanity in its grip with ecological devastation, war and racism/misogyny growing stronger. Russell Means saw this continuing bad behavior as proof that Europeans were unable to hear the call to respect nature. OK, I said to myself, so now what? There is no magic button or pill to change all of this. Whether we like it or not, we live in continuum with our past.

Marxism and materialism alone did not provide me with an adequate explanation of the human crises we are living through. Despiritualizing reality has locked us into the destructive path of modern life. How would bringing the Goddess back into human awareness change things?

I had to make a distinction between consciousness and spirituality. Consciousness is like an appendage, an arm or a leg, that we all have and that define us as human beings. Spirituality enters our consciousness when we become aware of the spirit world in everything around us. Monotheistic religions of private property may limit our consciousness. But we all still witness the spiritual nature of the universe. In prehistory, when a family found itself displaced from their homelands, living under a bridge so to speak, and out in the cold, this had a large impact on their consciousness. It did the job of limiting consciousness and separating us from the spirit world. We had to adapt to a world that was out of sic with nature. Survival led us astray.

I admit that our stubborn adherence to patriarchy cannot be separated from our spirituality. Patriarchy is reborn generation after generation like that movie "Groundhog Day" keeps repeating the same day over and over. In the movie, (spoiler alert!), he finds love and wakes up the next day. I wish it were that simple. But it is not.

Religious people might say that if we discover God, we will change. Yet from what I have seen, discovering God is just the beginning of religious war and the opposite of a solution. Monotheism weds us to private property and its wars. Since ancient times Goddess worshipers displaced from their clan and their land have converted to monotheism as a way to join the conquerors. Inmates discover Jesus to get out of jail. The choice has not changed. Some God in the sky did not give us our spiritual nature. Our spiritual nature gave us God.

Love exists in the patriarchal world as surely as it does in the non property owning world. But it does not rid us of our attachment to private property. Nor does it end the war against women.

Russell Means statement that Europeans have proven ourselves unable to hear the message that we must live in harmony with the Earth comes down to our allegiance to private property. From the very first time a man ripped off the land from his mother's clan until now, private ownership has poisoned the civilized mind. The hegemonic ideology of private property is reborn anew every generation as children witness it in their mother's dependency on their father's power, in their siblings play, and in their relationships with people (rich and poor) outside the nuclear family. Above all, children witness it in their relationship to the land. We no longer know the land or the names of the creeks and rivers. No one explains how we preserve the Earth and revere the waters that flow around us. Instead, we walk on concrete surfaces, no mud on our shoes. We live in a world designed by architects that hides the natural world, creating the illusion that nothing exists outside the human melodrama. The countryside continues to empty into the cities not to flee nature, but rather to flee the social constraints and poverty created by private property.

In the growth of modern urbanization, humanity left the natural world behind. The bright lights hypnotize the wanderers promising fame and fortune for the lucky ones. Our connections to the Earth, to any single place, are broken. We have evolved into a society in which the most comfortable chair we have is the driver's seat in our cars. The Earth is now a spectacle for an audience to view as we speed by, racking up points on a bucket list of things we have seen but never really known. When all along, we are blind to the here and now and no longer know anything about a single place on the planet.

How do we move away from this alienated and destructive way of life? Revolution? Evolution?

Voting? Only when we understand the necessity to modify private ownership of land and property will we open the path towards respecting nature. Socialism offers many promises, but when state property is substituted for private property we run into the same dead end. Russell Means refusal to be proletarianized, to give up his culture or his land in order to join the working classes, dramatizes this dilemma.

Today some 25% of the Earth's surface is still in the hands of indigenous people.[79] Russell Means admonition to evaluate any proposal for change by its impact on the non-European, non-civilized people remains the best critical focus I can find. Recognizing indigenous land rights is the first step. Giving water, rivers and oceans the right to be clean and healthy is equally important. Until we embrace the implications of the prehistoric origins of human culture, centered on women, living in harmony with nature, and without property ownership or war, will we begin to move towards a sustainable way of life.

My Journey

My journey started with Russell Means' challenge to hear what the tribes had been telling us to respect the Earth. First I realized that his challenge could not be met by words alone. No matter how much I might try, I could not change my settler culture to respect nature and live in harmony with the Earth. Through my contact with tribes in the southwest, I realized that there were alternatives to the western rationalism that I grew up with. This insight came to me as a youth in high school and then grew larger over the years. I began to see that the problem lay deeply in the way we live, in the structure of our families, neighborhoods, and our society. I wondered how did we get this way? I asked myself was there ever a time when my ancestors, my people, white people, lived in harmony with nature? My search through history led me to conclude that there was no time in our history when we lived in harmony with nature. Prehistory might be different. So I started to examine it.

The first thing that became apparent was that prehistory dwarfed history. Prehistory was measured in millennia. Thousands of years. History is measured in decades and centuries. Second, after sifting through the male bias in the study of prehistory, it was clear to me that prehistoric human societies worldwide were all characterized by matrilineal and matrilocal cultures. These two terms are more accurate than the term matriarchy because human existence was not ruled by power relations in prehistory. There is no evidence of war in prehistory. This concept is key to understanding it.

Prehistory is the period after the evolutionary emergence of our species, homo sapiens, and before writing. So looking at prehistory in this long view, I came upon the writings of Marija Gimbutas, Monica Sjoo, Barbara Mor and others. They convinced me that the millenniums of prehistory were woman centered. They showed me how human evolution hinged on the changes in the female anatomy to allow for the birth of human babies with our big brains. Male anatomy did not change for 3 million years. But female anatomy did change especially in the last 500,000 years. And with these changes came the essential characteristics of our species. Social life became part of the birth process. Language and group life became the means of survival of the species, and wove its way into our genetic make up with the changes in the tongue, the brain, the facial muscles, etc.

Before civilization ever wrote down a single word, human beings lived all over the planet numbering in the millions. The woman centered clans who lived on the land without owning it created all the essential tools of modern homo sapiens. Everything from cloth, pottery, tools, domesticated animals and plants to the settled village life grew out of the wandering hunters and gatherers of our origins. Within this millenniums-long period of prehistory arose the male seizure of the land claiming it as private property and losing sight of the Earth as our mother.

The rise of private property in male hands could only have succeeded by instituting the subjugation of women as the wife, the legal chattel, the slave of the male property owners. Women were not only enslaved sexually, but also as workers doing the age old tasks of supplying humanity with the food we eat. This change grew within human societies all over the planet giving rise to war and conquest. Classes arose defined by wealth accumulation based on ownership. Powerful states arose from associations of property owners until the arrival of empires and civilizations with their writings and new monotheistic gods.

Civilization has now reached the end of the line. Human ownership of the land, coupled with the subjugation of women are now destroying the natural balances out of which humanity arose. Climate change with its fires, floods and mass extinctions is now rebounding upon human life globally as nature reasserts the balances we have destroyed. As the natural crisis mounts in severity, human greed and the quest for riches continues to drive us further and further towards disaster.

If the roots of our global rush to disaster are in patriarchy and private property, what does humanity, now 8 billion strong, do to turn this around? I have my answers to this question and so do many others who have thought about it. Whatever happens, it is clearly necessary for us to heed the call of Russell Means and others to respect nature and the earth. Human societies must take off the patriarchal blinders and recognize fundamental rights to women and the earth to exist in a healthy condition. At a minimum, this means reforming the laws on property rights to include the rights of rivers to be clean, of other life forms to live free of poisons and extinction, of the air to be clean and breathable. The right of women to control their own bodies, including the right to abortion, is the bottom line in the fight to reform patriarchy. The expansion of the social safety networks to include child care, free education, and to put an end homelessness, give expression to the social compact that must replace the individualism that has led us down the wrong path. We cannot pull these elements apart and solve them piece by piece. They are all related and the success of any part depends on the advancement of the whole.

Patriarchy will not give up easily. Controlling the earth for private profit or other selfish human ends will not be easy to stop. But respecting nature and protecting the right of women to control their own bodies is the same issue. Our relationship to the earth, our lack of respect and love for her, is based on private ownership which gives humans the right to do any rotten thing we want to the earth. That will be hard to change.

Can Marxism give up its adherence to the notions of savagery, barbarism and civilization? Can Marxism embrace the spiritual nature of the earth and our connection to it and therefore find a way to join the struggles of the dispossessed with the struggles of the indigenous people? Or are these two different world views incompatible with each other? Can we find a pathway to adapt the modern world to the age old truths of our Goddess prehistory that might put us on a path to sustainability? Certainly there is no going back to prehistory and no immediate prospect of abolishing private property that presents itself as any kind of a realistic solution in the immediate future. But just asking these questions suggests that answers are out there.

Looking at the current imbalances between the rich and the poor in the world today blinds us to the fact that urban industrial civilization has produced the most incredible surpluses the world has ever seen. The scarcity imposed upon humanity along with the degradation of the planet come from the hold of private property on all civilizations. This imbalance is not because of overpopulation or human nature. If humanity modifies private property laws in favor of the common good and sustainability, it is obvious that scarcity could be abolished. Just like hunger could be abolished along with the waste in the food systems that now exist. Ecological harm could be removed from human activities equally obviously. We have the knowledge and the methods to do it. We just do not have the will or understanding. What stands in the way is private property and patriarchy, buttressed by monotheistic religions that blind us to the alternatives. Finding acceptance and understanding of this basic fact of the modern world opens the door to our transformation.

Endnotes

Part 1

1. Russell Means, "For America to Live, Europe Must Die," , 1980. https://theanarchistlibrary.org/library/russell-means-for-america-to-live-europe-must-die

2. Means, "For America to Live."

Part 2

3. See https://www.npr.org/2020/11/20/937009453/the-cias-secret-quest-for-mind-control-torture-lsd-and-a-poisoner-in-chief for more on this sad story.

4. John Neihardt, *Black Elk Speaks*, Bison Books 2014, page 121.

5. Neihardt, *Black Elk*, page 1-2

6. Neihardt, *Black Elk*, page 23

7. Sizani Ngubane, "The Rural Women's Movement in South Africa," *Women and the Gift Economy, a Radically Different Worldview Is Possible*, edited by Genevieve Vaughan.

Part 3

8. Marija Gimbutas, *Civilization of the Goddess,* HarperCollins 1991, page vii..

9. Gimbutas, *Civilization*, page viii.

10. Sjöö, Monica; Mor, Barbara. *The Great Cosmic Mother: Rediscovering the Religion of the Earth.* HarperCollins. Kindle Edition, page 7.

11. Sjöö and Mor, *Cosmic Mother*, page 25-26.

12. Sjöö and Mor, *Cosmic Mother*, page 11-12.

Part 4

13. Means, "For America to Live."

14. https://estuarypress.com/hrma-blog-post/the-photographic-adventures/

15. https://youtu.be/zvwRZ3H5orE.

16. https://estuarypress.com/hrma-blog-post/about-harvey-richards/.

17. https://estuarypress.com/

18. https://estuarypress.com/wp-content/uploads/2020/12/HR-Media-Archive-Archival-Holdings-2016_05_01-18_07_06-UTC.pdf

19. https://estuarypress.com/harvey-richards-media-archive-home/photo-galleries/.

20. see https://estuarypress.com/hrma-blog-post/the-photographic-adventures/.

21. https://estuarypress.com/book/critical-focus/

22. https://estuarypress.com/nina-serrano-homepage/poetry/

23. https://estuarypress.com/estuary-press-home/multi-media-publications/estuary-press-book-store/

24. https://estuarypress.com/nina-serrano-homepage/

25. https://estuarypress.com/

26. https://estuarypress.com/harvey-richards-media-archive-home/

27. https://www.youtube.com/channel/UCjLntHEno-2ygOiD0fOl0Aw

28. https://estuarypress.com/hrma-blog-post/licensing-history-1987-2013/

29. https://estuarypress.com/harvey-richards-media-archive-home/soviet-union-photography/

30. https://estuarypress.com/ep-blog-post/the-left-side-of-history/

31. https://estuarypress.com/ep-blog-post/book-review-this-nonviolent-stuffll-get-you-killed-by-charles-e-cobb-jr/

32. Engels, Friedrich, *Origins of the Family, Private Property and the State*, Online Version: Marx/Engels Internet Archive (marxists.org) 1993, 1999, 2000, page 87.

33. Engels, *Origins*, page 87

34. Marija Gimbutas, *The Living Goddesses*, University of California Press 1999, Kindle Edition, page 52.

35. Gimbutas, *Living Goddesses*, page 52.

Part 5

36. Hamilton, Edith. *Mythology, Timeless Tales of Gods and Heroes,* Hachette Book Group, Black Dog & Leventhal Purblishers, 2017, page 1

37. Hamilton, *Mythology*, page 2.

38. Hamilton, *Mythology, page 2.*

39. Hesiod, "Theogeny", *in Anthology of Classical Myth: Primary Sources in Translation*, edited by Thomas Palaima, *Hackett Publishing Company, Inc.. Kindle Edition, p 134*

40. Hesiod, "Theogeny" in *Anthology*, page 135.

41. Hesiod, "Theogeny" in *Anthology*, page 135.

42. Hesiod, "Theogeny" in *Anthology*, page 136.

43. Hesiod, "Theogeny" in *Anthology*, pages 136 -137.

44. Hesiod, "Theogeny" in *Anthology*, pages 138.

45. Apollodorus, "The Early Gods" the Rise of Zeus, *Anthology,* p. 18

46. "Homeric Hymns", "To Demeter", *Anthology*, page 170.

47. "Homeric Hymns", in *Anthology*, p. 171.

48. "Homeric Hymns", in *Anthology*, p. 171.

49. "Homeric Hymns", in *Anthology*, p. 172.

50. "Homeric Hymns", in *Anthology*, p. 174.

51. "Homeric Hymns", in *Anthology*, p. 175.

52. "Homeric Hymns", in *Anthology*, p. 176.

53 "Homeric Hymns", in *Anthology*, p. 176.

54 "Homeric Hymns", in *Anthology*, p. 176.

55. "Homeric Hymns", in *Anthology*, p. 178.

56. Apollodorus, "The Early Gods," in *Anthology*, pages 162-163.

57. Sjöö and Mor, *Cosmic Mother*, page 11-12

58. Apollodorus, "The Early Gods," in *Anthology*, page 163.

59. Apollodorus, "The Early Gods," in *Anthology*, pages 163-164.

60. Apollodorus, "The Early Gods," in *Anthology*, page 164.

61. Apollodorus, "The Early Gods," in *Anthology*, page 164.

62. Ovid's Metamorphoses,
https://en.wikipedia.org/wiki/Golden_Age#cite_note-7

63. Apollodorus, "The Early Gods," in *Anthology*, page 165.

64. Apollodorus, "The Early Gods," in *Anthology*, page 165.

65. Apollodorus, "The Early Gods," in *Anthology*, page 165.

66. Apollodorus, "The Early Gods," in *Anthology*, page 167.

Part 6

67. *Genesis 1, Bible Gateway, New International Version*
https://www.biblegateway.com/passage/?search=Genesis%202%3A4-3%3A24&version=NIV

68. *Genesis 1.*

69. *Genesis 1.*

70. *Genesis 2.*

71. *Genesis 2.*

72. *Genesis* 2.

73. Genesis 2-3.

74. Gimbutas, *Living Goddess*, p. 14.

75. Genesis 3

76. Genesis 3,

77. Genesis 3,

78. Gimbutas, Civilization, Preface, page x.

Part 7

79. https://www.researchgate.net/figure/Global-map-of-lands-managed-and-or-controlled-by-Indigenous-Peoples-percentage-of-each_fig1_326424629

Bibliography

Adovaslo, J.M., and Olga Soffer, & Jake Page. *The Invisible Sex, Uncovering the True Roles of Women in Prehistory.* HarperCollins e-books, 2007. Kindle.

Anderson, M. Kat. *Tending the Wild: Native American Knowledge and the Management of California's Natural Resources.* Berkeley/Los Angeles/London: University of California Press, 2005. Kindle.

Bible Gateway. New International Version, http://www.biblegateweay.com/passage/.

Brown, Joseph Epes. *The Sacred Pipe, Black Elk's Account of the Seven Rites of the Oglala Sioux.* Norman: University of Oklahoma Press, 1953,1989. Kindle.

Brown, Joseph Epes. *The Spiritual Legacy of the American Indian.* Bloomington: World Wisdon, 2007. Kindle.

Engels, Friedrich. *Origin of the Family, Private Property, and the State.* Online Version: Marx/Engels Internet Archive (marxists.org), 1993, 1999, 2000.

Fischer, John Ryan. *Cattle Colonialism: An Environmental History of the Conquest of California and Hawai'a.* Chapel Hill: University of North Carolina Press, 2015. Kindle.

Ghodsee, Kristen R.. *Second World, Second Sex.* Durham: Duke University Press, 2019. Kindle.

Ghodsee, Kristen R.. *The Left Side of History, World War II and the Unfulfilled Promise of Communism in Eastern Europe.* Durham and London: Duke University Press, 2015. Kindle.

Ghodsee, Kristen R.. *Why Women Have Better Sex Under Socialism, and Other Arguments for Economic Independence.* New York: Nation Books, 2018. Kindle.

Ghodsee, Kristen R.. *Red Valkyries: Feminist Lessons from Fiver Revolutionary Women*. London/New York: Verso, 2022. Kindle.

Gimbutas, Marija. *The Living Goddesses*. Edited and Supplemented by Miriam Robbins Dexter. Berkeley/Los Angeles/London: University of California Press 2001. Kindle.

Gimbutas, Marija. *The Civilization of the Goddess, The World of Old Europe*. Edited by Joan Marler. San Francisco: HarperSanFrancisco, 1991.

Graeber, David and Wengrow, David. *The Beginning of Everything: A New History of Humanity*. New York, NY: Farrar, Straus and Giroux, 2021.

Hamilton, Edith. *Mythology: Timeless Tales of Gods and Heroes*. New York: Black Dopg & Leventhal Publishers, 2017. Kindle.

Haynes, Matalie. *Pandora's Jar, Women in Greek Myths*. London: Picador, 2020.

Hoskins, W.G.. *The Making of the English Landscape*. London: Hodder & Stoughton, 1955.

Kuhn, Thomas S. *The Structure of Scientific Revolutions*. Chicago: University of Chicago Press, 1962.

Lerner, Gerda. The Creation of Patriarchy. New York: Oxford University Press, 1986.

Manco, Jean. *Ancestral Journeys: The Peopling of Europe from Venturers to the Vikings*. London: Thames & Hudson Ltd., 2013. Kindle.

Neihardt, John G.. *Black Elk Speaks*, Lincoln and London: Bison Books, 2014. Kindle.

Nelson, Sarah Milledge. *Gender in Archaeology: Analyzing Power and Prestige*. Maryland: AltaMira Press, 2004. Kindle.

Nelson, S.D.. *Black Elk's Vision: A Lakota Story*. New York: Abrams Illustrated Edition, 2010. Kindle.

Nelson, Sarah Milledge, editor. *Women in Antiquity, Theoretical Approaches to Gender and Archaeology.* Plymouth, UK: AltaMira Press 2007. Kindle.

Palaima, Thomas G.. *Anthology of Classical Myth: Primary Sources in Translation.* Translated by Stephen M. Trzaskoma, R. Scot Smith, Stephen Brunet. Indianapolis/Cambridge: Hackett Publishing, 2004. Kindle.

Pearson, Mike Parker. Stonehenge, A New Understanding. New York: The Experiment, 2013. Kindle.

Proudhon, Pierre-Joseph. *Works of Pierre-Joseph Proudhon.* The Perfect Library, 1888, 2010. Kindle.

Pryor, Francis. *Britain BC: Life in Britain and Ireland Before the Romans.* London: Harper Perennial 2004. Kindle.

Pryor, Francis. *Home: A Time Traveller's Tales from Britain's Prehistory.* London: Penguin Group, 2014. Kindle.

Pryor, Francis. *The Making of the British Landscape: How We have Transformed the Land from Prehistory to Today.* London: Penguin Group, 2011. Kindle.

Pryor, Francis. *Seahenge: a quest for life and death in Bronze Age Britain.* London: HarperPress, 2001. Kindle.

Pryor, Francis. *Britain AD: A Quest for Arthur, England and the Anglo-Saxons.* London: Harper Press, 2004. Kindle.

Scott, James c. *Against the Grain, A Deep History of the Earliest States.* New Haven: Yale University Press, 2017.

Secrest, William B.. *When the Great Spirit Died: The Destruction of the California Indians 1850 – 1860.* Sanger, CA: Word Dancer Press, 2003. Kindle.

Shlain, Leonard. The Alphabet Versus the Goddess: The Conflict Between Word and Image. New York: Penguin Group, 1998. Kindle.

Sjöö, Monica and Barbara Mor. *The Great Cosmic Mother: Rediscovering the Religion of the Earth.* San Francisco: Harper & Row, 1987. Kindle.

Specter, Janet. *What This Awl Means, Feminist Archaeology at a Wahpeton Dakota Village.* St. Paul: Minnesota Historical Society Press, 1993. Kindle.

Stone, Merlin. *When God Was a Woman.* New York: The Dial Press, 1976. Kindle.

Sykes, Brian. *The Seven Daughters of Ever: The Science That Reveals Our Genetic Ancestry.* New York: W.W. Norton & Company, 2002. Kindle.

Tippett, Constance. *Goddess Timeline,* https://youtu.be/th0gEh1xpjg.

Vaughan, Genevieve. *Women and the Gift Economy: A Radically Different Worldview is Possible.* Toronto: Inanna Publications, 2007. Kindle.

William Appleman Williams. *The Contours of American History.* New York: W.W. Norton & Company, 1989.

Yunkaporta, Tyson. *Sand Talk: How Indigenous Thinking Can Save the World.* San Francisco, California: Harper One, 2020.

All human beings are descendants of tribal people who were spiritually alive, intimately in love with the natural world, children of Mother Earth. When we were tribal people, we knew who we were, we knew where we were, and we knew our purpose. This sacred perception of reality remains alive and well in our genetic memory. We carry it inside of us, usually in a dusty box in the mind's attic, but it is accessible.

John Trudell

www.ingramcontent.com/pod-product-compliance
Lightning Source LLC
Chambersburg PA
CBHW051511150726
47997CB00001B/196